THE INDUSTRIAL REVOLUTION

THE INDUSTRIAL REVOLUTION

MILESTONES IN BUSINESS HISTORY

JEFF HORN

Greeenwood Press
Westport, Connecticut • London

Library of Congress Cataloging-in-Publication Data

Horn, Jeff, Ph. D.
    The Industrial Revolution / Jeff Horn.
        p.   cm. — (Milestones in business history, ISSN 1934–7251)
    Includes bibliographical references and index.
    ISBN 978–0–313–33853–3 (alk. paper)
    1. Industrial revolution—Great Britain—History.   2. Industrialization—Great
    Britain—History.   3. Great Britain—Economic conditions—History.   4. Industrial
    revolution—Europe.   5. Europe—Economic conditions—History.   I. Title.
    HC254.5.H67   2007
    330.941'07—dc22   2007000422

British Library Cataloguing in Publication Data is available.

Library of Congress Catalog Card Number: 2007000422
ISBN–13: 978–0–313–33853–3
ISBN–10: 0–313–33853–1
ISSN: 1934–7251

First published in 2007

Greenwood Press, 88 Post Road West, Westport, CT 06881
An imprint of Greenwood Publishing Group, Inc.
www.greenwood.com

Printed in the United States of America

The paper used in this book complies with the
Permanent Paper Standard issued by the National
Information Standards Organization (Z39.48–1984).

10 9 8 7 6 5 4 3 2 1

CONTENTS

PREFACE

The onset of the industrial revolution was not inevitable in its timing or location. This book traces how the Western countries led by Great Britain developed the means of industrializing their economies. As both cause and consequence of this economic development and the creation of an economic system that spanned the globe, over the course of the eighteenth and nineteenth centuries, the West became far richer, far more productive, and far more powerful than the rest of the world. It was the industrial revolution that opened the gap between "the West" and "the rest." Thus, an important part of the story of the industrial revolution is how the states of the West—through trade, conquest, and colonization—were able to appropriate the land, labor, and natural resources of other parts of the world for their own benefit.

Two other major analytic themes usually left out of accounts of industrialization underpin this book. The Western countries may have come to dominate other parts of the world, but domination for economic purposes began at home. Great Britain could initiate an industrial revolution because its entrepreneurs were able to enforce work rhythms, laboring conditions, and wage scales that would have provoked social revolution in all of its closest competitors. By transforming the relationship of the laboring classes to the industrial work process, British entrepreneurs, their imitators, and their competitors were able to earn phenomenal profits and generate wealth at an unprecedented rate. The interactions of management and labor complement the more common focus on technological innovation and the supply of new products in the account of industrialization elaborated here.

A third and final theme of this work is a focus on the historical role of the state in industrialization. All too frequently, theoretical assumptions about the nature of "laissez-faire" economics color examinations of the actual historical record. The state supported industrialization thoroughly with institutions like national banks, legal protections such as patents, by managing trade through the tariff and commercial treaties, and, when necessary, with force.

The Western powers repeatedly deployed their military might for economic purposes: arms were used to open markets, protect national interests, and to shelter domestic entrepreneurs by ensuring that the laboring classes could not topple the pillars of industrial society. Without defense by the state, Western entrepreneurs could not have initiated or maintained the industrial revolution.

This approach is dedicated to demonstrating the changes in business practice, the economic environment along with the roles of entrepreneurs, the state, and workers that took place during the industrial revolution. Economic and business history is not just stodgy statistics and dry descriptions of accounting practices. Whenever possible, people of the time speak in their own words. Quotes, documents, and biographies from businesspeople, laborers, and state officials reveal the lived responses of the past. Individuals created and reacted to the new forms of business organization, novel means of shaping production and overseeing labor, as well as to technological innovation. Shifts in perception and the human condition, illuminated through first-hand accounts and biographies of key figures, put a human face on the statistics and descriptions used to illuminate the depth of economic transformation.

The first chapter, "Growth and the Standard of Living in the Industrial Revolution," defines key terms and explains what differentiates an industrial revolution from other forms of economic growth. This chapter also explores some common misconceptions about the industrial revolution that have crept into many business and economic histories. These fallacies distort contemporary understandings of the lessons of the industrial revolution for modern business practice.

Chapter 2, "The Building Blocks of a New Economy," sets the stage for industrialization. Over the course of centuries, the nations of Western Europe created conditions in which an industrial revolution could emerge. From agriculture to transport to colonization to the role of the stage, entrepreneurs participated in and encountered the results of the formation of a fundamentally different economic environment. The opportunities these individuals took advantage of and created demonstrate what conditions were necessary for the modern process of industrialization to commence.

The third chapter, "Making an Industrial Revolution I: Technological Change," explores the key innovations in the leading industrial sectors of cotton, iron, and coal. The role of supply and demand in inducing technological innovation will be explored through the actions of important tinkerers and inventors. Although they were scientifically dependent on continental Europe, the British were technologically preeminent, which helps to explain why that country was the first to industrialize.

Chapter 4, "Making an Industrial Revolution II: The Elaboration of the Factory System," parallels the previous chapter by demonstrating the revolutionary changes in business organization and the oversight of labor. These shifts were just as important to the success of industrialization as technological innovation. Without the emergence of more efficient means of production, the industrial revolution would have been stillborn.

"Why Was Britain First?" is the subject of the fifth chapter. The material resources, geographical advantages, and technological prowess of Great Britain were sufficient conditions to permit industrial development. However, the truly necessary factory in turning these conditions from potential into actual industrial growth was the intervention of the British state to ensure that the heavy-handed style of labor management that made this model of industrialization possible was not disrupted by social revolution. "Laissez-faire" economics was never and could not be practiced during the age of the industrial revolution.

The sixth chapter, "Leads and Lags: Competing with a Dominant Economic Power," applies the model of British industrialization developed in the previous chapters and applies them to the experiences of the first generation of industrial "followers." France, the United States, Belgium, and the German lands all had different means of industrializing. Their examples prove that deviation from a model is often necessary. Entrepreneurs and state officials developed distinctive relationships that shed light on the importance of business decision making and how economic and business "rationality" worked in different times and different places to forge an industrial revolution.

Chapter 7, "Industrialization and the New World Order," explicitly demonstrates the exploitative nature of the process of industrialization. The creation of a world economic system centered on Europe permitted the West to siphon wealth from the rest of the globe. This chapter explores how essential imperialism and colonization were to maintaining industrial growth and economic prosperity. The growing political and social influence of Europe's laboring classes made finding other people to overwork an essential part of maximizing profits. Without this high level of Western control, the industrial revolutions of the nineteenth century would have been far slower and less powerful—if they would have occurred at all.

The final chapter, "Demand, Supply, and the Fickle Whims of Fashion," examines the changes in how and what people consumed. Entrepreneurs found or created myriad new opportunities to supply the goods demanded by the burgeoning middle classes. The ability to make different goods more cheaply often took a back seat to innovations in advertising, marketing, and distribution. The product competition of this period represented the genesis of many facets of modern business practice.

The Industrial Revolution attempts to demonstrate to modern readers the historical origins of the current global economy. At the same time, by focusing on the individual and collective decisions that, taken together, "made" the industrial revolution, this account demonstrates the practical limitations of models and economic theory. Finally, as the so-called "Third World" attempts to catch up with the advanced Western economies, this historical chronicle of how the West got rich has many lessons for those interested in contemporary economic development. Without understanding why and how the industrial revolution took place, it is impossible to comprehend the pace, timing, and nature of long-term economic change in the last 250 years.

ACKNOWLEDGMENTS

The structure of this book owes a great deal to the vision of former editor Nick Philipson at Greenwood who conceived the outline for the series. I am deeply grateful and indebted to my colleague at Manhattan College, Charles Geisst, for making the introduction to Nick. The Burndy Library of the Dibner Institute for the History of Science and Technology at the Massachusetts Institute of Technology made finding the images a pleasure. Philip Cronenwett, the director, Howard Kennett, the technical services librarian, and the entire staff were generous with their time and extraordinarily helpful. John Gormley, the Interlibrary Loan librarian at the Mary Alice and Tom O'Malley Library of Manhattan College, tracked down a number of useful books. Richard Musal adapted the maps with his usual efficiency and verve. Len Rosenband was, as always, a valuable sounding board and cheerleader, as I worked my way through all this material. He also provided helpful readings of key chapters. Many years ago, from the vantage point of her research assistant, Lynn Hunt taught me a great deal about organizing this kind of project. My wife Julie has been tolerant as the house filled up with dusty tomes on obscure topics and accepted my general air of distraction while writing. This book is dedicated to my children David and Cate: this is the kind of history book I hope they will enjoy reading.

CHRONOLOGY

1651	Passage of the English Navigation Act.
1660	English Royal Society founded.
1687	Isaac Newton publishes major work.
1688	Glorious Revolution in England.
1689	English Corn Law enacted.
1694	Bank of England formed.
1707	Act of Union between England and Scotland to form Great Britain.
1712	Thomas Newcomen's steam engine first used.
1714	House of Hanover comes to power in England under George I.
1742	Benjamin Huntsman discovers how to make cast or crucible steel.
1751	Publication of the first volume (of 24) of the *Encyclopédie* of Denis Diderot and Jean le Rond d'Alembert, finished in 1772.
1753	British colonist Benjamin Franklin invents the lightning conductor in Philadelphia.
1754	Foundation of the Royal Society of Arts in London.
1761	Bridgewater Canal opens.
1764	Englishman James Hargreaves invents the spinning jenny. It is patented six years later.

1769	Patents issued for Richard Arkwright's water frame, James Hargreaves' spinning jenny, and James Watt's separate condenser for steam engines.
1775–1783	War for American Independence.
1776	Publication of Adam Smith's *Wealth of Nations.*
1776	Turgot's Six Acts implemented in France.
1779	Samuel Crompton develops the spinning mule.
1783	Brothers Étienne and Joseph Montgolfier inaugurate hot-air balloon travel in Annonay, France.
1784	Englishman Henry Cort develops the puddling process for wrought iron.
1784	Frenchman Claude Berthollet develops a method for chemical bleaching.
1784	The British "drawback"—a bounty on exports—enacted.
1784–1786	Edmund Cartwright invents the power loom in England, it is patented in stages.
1785	Arkwright's water frame patent overturned.
1786	Anglo-French Commercial Treaty.
1789	Outbreak of the French Revolution. Extensive machine-breaking takes place.
1790	Establishment of U.S. patent system in law.
1790	Samuel Slater establishes first textile factory in the United States.
1792–1802	French Revolutionary wars.
1793	American Eli Whitney develops the cotton gin.
1793–1794	Reign of Terror in France.
1794	Creation of the National Institute and the Polytechnic in Paris.
1798	First industrial exposition held in Paris.
1799	Englishman Charles Tennant creates bleaching powder.
1799–1814, 1815	Napoleon Bonaparte rules France.

1799–1800	Two English Combination Acts forbid collective activity by workers.
1800	Italian Alessandro Volta invents a means of storing electricity in a battery composed of zinc and copper plates.
1800	Englishman Richard Trevithick constructs a new model steam engine based on higher steam pressures.
1800–1804	Jean-Antoine Chaptal serves as Minister of the Interior in France.
1801	Joseph-Marie Jacquard perfects a loom to weave silk.
1801	Society for the Encouragement of the National Industry founded in Paris.
1801	Union of Great Britain with Ireland to form the United Kingdom.
1803–1814, 1815	Napoleonic wars.
1806–1813	French Continental System in place.
1807	American Robert Fulton's *Clermont* travels from New York City to Albany.
1807–1815	American embargo on British goods.
1809–1814	Abrogation of paternalist protections for workers in the United Kingdom.
1811–1817	Luddites break machines in the United Kingdom.
1812–1815	War of 1812 between the United States and the United Kingdom.
1813	Boston Manufacturing Company formed, led by Francis Cabot Lowell.
1815	Treaty of Vienna ends the Napoleonic wars. Prussia receives the Ruhr, Belgium is given to the Kingdom of the Netherlands, and France loses its conquests of a generation.
1818	Prussia founds the Zollverein, a customs union.
1819	English Factory Act passes ineffective restrictions on child labor.
1820	Quinine extracted from cinchona bark.

1821	Gold standard established by the United Kingdom to support the currency.
1822	The first mill at Lowell established by the Boston Manufacturing Company.
1824	Repeal of the English Combination Acts and the restrictions on the emigration of skilled workers.
1825	George Stephenson develops an effective steam locomotive from his first prototype of 1814.
1825	Richard Robert's self-acting mule patented.
1825	Opening of the Erie Canal.
1825	Justus von Liebig opens the first modern research laboratory at Giessen.
1829	British chemist James Smithson leaves a fortune to found the Smithsonian Institution in Washington, DC.
1829–1833	Machine-breaking in the United Kingdom.
1830	Revolutions of 1830. Belgium becomes independent.
1833	English Factory Act prohibiting the employment of children under age 9 and limiting that for older children.
1833	Slavery prohibited in the British Empire.
1837	English scientist Charles Wheatstone develops the telegraph.
1839–1842	First Opium War between the United Kingdom and China.
1844	Samuel F.B. Morse patents an alphabetic code for telegraphy in the United States.
1844	Outbreak of machine-breaking in the Prussian province of Silesia.
1846	Repeal of the Corn Laws in the United Kingdom.
1848	Revolutions of 1848.
1848	Slavery outlawed in the French Empire.
1849	Repeal of the Navigation Laws.
1850	Opening of the Britannia Bridge over the Menai Straits.
1851	The International Exhibition featuring the Crystal Palace opens in London.
1856–1860	Second Opium War between the United Kingdom and China.

1857–1858	Mutiny of elements of the British Indian Army.
1860	Anglo-French Commercial Treaty.
1865	Slavery outlawed in the United States.
1871	Unification of Germany complete.
1884	American Hiram Maxim develops the first practical single-barrel, rapid-fire machine gun.
1914–1918	First World War.

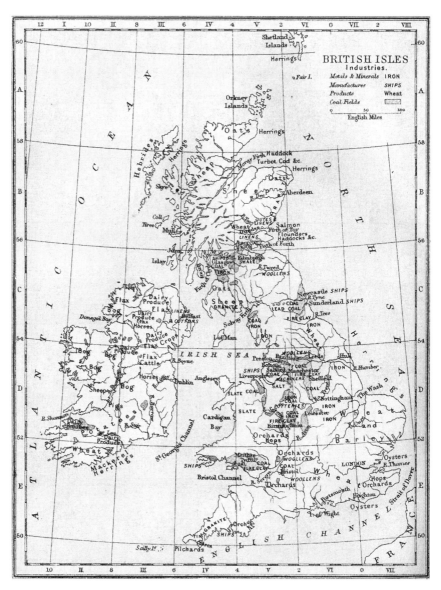

The major industrial sites of the late nineteenth century along with centers for certain industrial products and where natural resources were to be found. *Source: British Isles: Industries.* From Samuel Rawson Gardiner, ed., *A School Atlas of English History* (London: Longmans, 1892), 64.

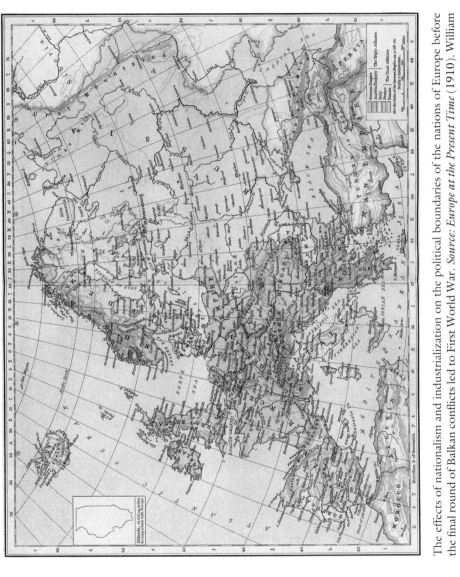

The effects of nationalism and industrialization on the political boundaries of the nations of Europe before the final round of Balkan conflicts led to First World War. *Source: Europe at the Present Time* (1910). William Sheperd, ed., *Historical Atlas* (New York: Henry Holt, 1911), 166–167.

COLONIZING ACTIVITIES OF MODERN EUROPE

Adapted By: Richard A. Musal

The enormous extent of European empires on the eve of the First World War. Note both the vastness of British territories and the expansion of all European possessions since the eighteenth century and the dawn of the industrial revolution. *Source: Colonizing Activities of Modern Europe.* Based on Ernest John Knapton and Thomas Kingston Derry, *Europe, 1815–1914* (New York: Charles Scribner's Sons, 1966), 300–301. Adapted by Richard A. Musal.

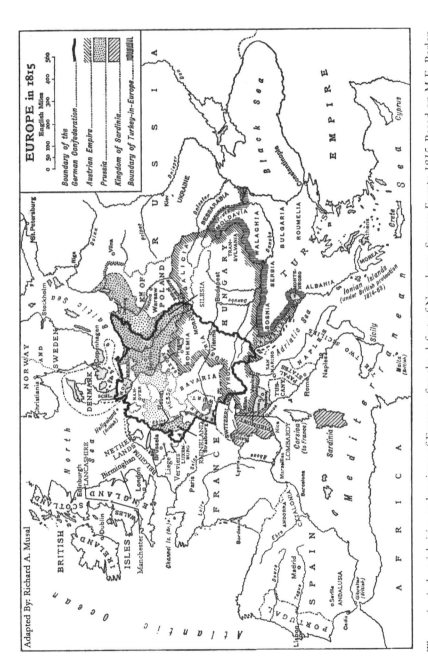

The major industrial cities and regions of Europe after the defeat of Napoleon. *Source: Europe 1815.* Based on M.E. Barlen, *The Foundations of Modern Europe 1789–1871* (London: G. Bell and Sons, 1968), 165. Adapted by Richard A. Musal.

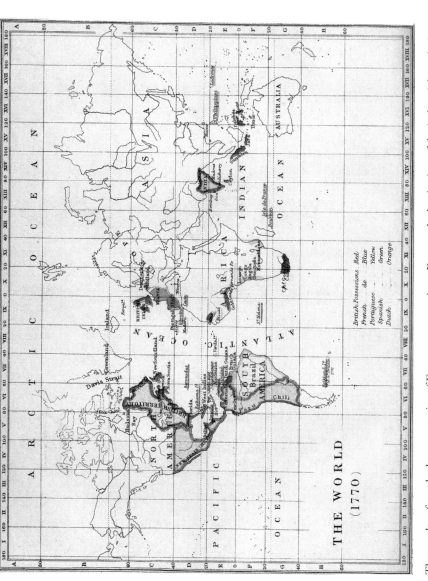

The results of nearly three centuries of European expansion. Even at the beginning of the industrial revolution, the British Empire was the largest in the world. *Source: The World (1772). From Charles Colbeck, ed., Public Schools Historical Atlas* (Longman's, Green and Company, 1905), 76.

1

GROWTH AND THE STANDARD OF LIVING IN THE INDUSTRIAL REVOLUTION

DEFINITIONS AND INTERPRETATIONS

What is an industrial revolution? Do we know it when we see it? More than 50 years ago, T.S. Ashton provided the most widely accepted definition of this vital historical process. The process began in Great Britain[1] late in the eighteenth century and, in the decades that followed, spread from there to many other places. Ashton identified five characteristics that differentiated an industrial "revolution" from other, less significant, forms of economic growth. The large-scale changes that Ashton's definition focused on were increased population, the application of science to industry, a more intensive and extensive use of capital, the conversion of rural to urban communities, and the rise of new social classes. From this list, demographic developments would appear to take pride of place over more purely economic shifts or the emergence of new technologies, yet it was Ashton's depiction of the development of a "wave of gadgets that swept Britain" during the industrial revolution that penetrated most deeply, thereby privileging technological change in most historical accounts.[2] This volume will explore these demographic, economic, and technological issues at length, but will place these factors in a broader context that also emphasizes the role of the state and the importance of empire to making an industrial revolution. All these subjects will be considered from the perspective of the daily life of those individuals—workers, bureaucrats, and entrepreneurs—who experienced the changes associated with industrialization in order to demonstrate how these large processes affected business decision making.

By characterizing the industrial revolution in somewhat vague economic, demographic, and technological terms that are applicable to different times and different places, this account will avoid misinterpretations of the historical record commonly found in business histories and in economics. For example, business history accounts of the industrial revolution generally focus on developments like the emergence of the professional manager that actually took place more than a century later during the Second Industrial Revolution (see Chapter 6). Such a misconception distorts contemporary understandings of the process of industrialization. Recognizing the haphazard, provisional, and uncertain nature of the initial stages of the industrial revolution is essential to understanding the continuing relevance of this pathbreaking economic process for contemporary business decision making.

Thomas R. Malthus (1766–1834)
"An Essay on the Principles of Population"

Malthus grew up in Surrey, the son of a country gentleman. He attended Cambridge University and was ordained an Anglican minister in 1797. It was while serving as a curate that he wrote the first edition of the work excerpted below. It was published anonymously in 1798 but soon afterward, he decided to garner additional supporting materials. A second, greatly expanded and revised edition appeared in 1803 and four further editions appeared at regular intervals. In 1805, Malthus became a professor of economics. His main goal in writing the "Essay" was to demonstrate the need for moral restraint on reproduction, but his work also describes contemporary thinking on the potential limitations on British growth.

there are few states in which there is not a constant effort in the population to increase beyond the means of subsistence. This constant effort as constantly tends to subject the lower classes of society to distress, and to prevent any great melioration of their condition.

These effects, in the present state of society, seem to be produced in the following manner. We will suppose the means of subsistence in any country just equal to the easy support of the inhabitants. The constant effort towards population, which is found to act even in the most vicious societies, increases the number of people before the means of subsistence are increased. The food, therefore, which before supported eleven millions must now be divided among eleven millions and a half. The poor consequently must live much worse, and many of them be reduced to severe distress. The number of labourers also being above the proportion of work in the market, the price of labour must tend to fall, which the price of provisions would at the same time tend to rise. The labourer therefore must do more work to earn the same as he did before. During the season of distress, the discouragements to marriage and the difficulty of rearing a family are so great, that the progress of population is retarded.

A faithful history, including such particulars, would tend greatly to elucidate the manner in which the constant check upon population acts; and would probably prove the existence of the retrograde and progressive movements that have been mentioned; though the times of their vibration must necessarily be rendered irregular from the operation of many interrupting causes; such as, the introduction or failure of certain manufactures; a greater or less prevalent spirit of agricultural enterprise; years of plenty or years of scarcity; wars, sickly seasons, poor laws, emigrations, and other causes of a similar nature.*

* Reprinted in John Bowditch and Clement Ramsland, eds., *Voices of the Industrial Revolution: Selected Readings from the Liberal Economists and Their Critics* (Ann Arbor, MI: The University of Michigan Press, 1957), 49, 55–57.

Source: Thomas R. Malthus, "An Essay on the Principle of Population as It Affects the Future Improvement of Society," 4th ed., 1807.

Economic interpretations of the industrial revolution commonly misrepresent why and how the process of industrialization took place. Economists and far too many economic historians mistake theory for practice when they argue that the industrial revolution was the result of an increasing supply of goods, both consumer and capital, that was available at ever-cheaper prices. A supply-side explanation for an industrial revolution overemphasizes the role of technology in the initial stages of industrialization and is insufficiently based on the historical record.[3] Instead, the new forms of production that were fundamental to the industrial revolution must be understood as a means of overcoming the natural limits on population framed by available resources described by Thomas Malthus that had curbed earlier efforts to industrialize (see insert). As shall be demonstrated in Chapter 2, during the eighteenth century, demand was able to stimulate the economy more successfully than earlier endeavors because it could build on an essential set of important agricultural, commercial, and imperial developments that took place in preceding centuries.

As Ashton's definition suggests, the industrial revolution gave rise to a new organization of society—the emergence of new classes, urbanization, and an expanding population. Industrialization made possible rates of economic growth that vanquished demographic pressures for the foreseeable future. This achievement was, and is, enormously important in its own right, but the industrial revolution also led to dramatic and long-lasting improvements in the standard of living that underpin the affluence of the contemporary industrialized world. Taken together, these two achievements explain why the process of industrialization in the Western world in the late eighteenth and nineteenth centuries was so "revolutionary."

THE ACCOMPLISHMENTS OF THE
INDUSTRIAL REVOLUTION

RATES OF GROWTH

What rate of economic growth is necessary to earn the designation of "industrial revolution?" Economic historians and economists have debated this issue for decades. The impossibility of providing a definitive statistical answer stems from the difficulties of measuring the causes and effects of industrialization. It is almost universally agreed that Great Britain was the first country to experience an industrial revolution. Industrialization has been studied there more thoroughly than in any other place, but despite sustained historical attention, due to limitations in the sources, scholars cannot agree on the pace, scope, or timing of the beginnings of high levels of economic growth. The most convincing scholarly estimates of the percentages of annual growth in the rate of real output from manufacturing range from 1.24 to 2.61 for the period 1760–1780, from 2.7 to 4.4 for the era 1800–1830, and from 2.9 to

3.1 for 1830–1870. Overall, the growth of newly industrialized sectors accounted for nearly two-thirds of productivity growth in the British economy between 1780 and 1860. By the middle of the nineteenth century, Great Britain dominated the global market for the products of "modern" industry. During the middle third of the nineteenth century, Britain produced two-thirds of world output of "new technology" products. Britain furnished half the planet's iron and cotton textiles and mined two-thirds of its coal. Discounting for inflation, Britain's gross national product (GNP) increased fourfold between 1780 and 1850. The British share of world industrial production rose from 2% in 1750 to 4.3% in 1800 to 9.5% in 1830, and to nearly 20% in 1860. Thus, a relatively small island nation became the "workshop of the world," achieving a level of global economic dominance never seen before or since.[4]

SECTORS AND REGIONS

National and global economic statistics obscure the sectoral and regional character of industrialization. Certain key industries like cotton textiles and machine-building grew at stunning rates thanks to technological changes that improved the productivity of labor. In the key growth sector—cotton textiles—output increased more than fivefold, while prices fell 50% in the generation from 1815 to 1841. The value of cotton textile production skyrocketed from £600,000 in 1770 to £48.6 million in 1851 and then to £104.9 million in 1871. About 60% of this output was exported. This phenomenal growth was centered in the county of Lancashire that produced between 55% and 70% of British output. Textiles contributed 46% of the value added by British industry both in 1770 and in 1831, but cotton's share of that proportion grew from 2.6% to 22.1% and wool fell from 30.5% to 14.1%.[5] As a result of the industrial revolution, Lancashire went from being one of the poorest and most backward of England's counties to being the motor of industrialization. Historian Joseph Inikori states that, "There can be no doubt that an industrial revolution occurred in Lancashire between 1780 and 1850, no matter how the term is defined, and that the Industrial Revolution in England was first and foremost a Lancashire phenomenon." The woolen textile producing region of the West Riding in Yorkshire, the iron foundries and machine shops of the West Midlands, known as the "Black Country" to contemporaries because of the heavy concentration of coal use, and the Scottish Lowlands were the other key districts that pioneered the industrial revolution in Great Britain. An extremely high percentage of the "modern" industries developed by Britain during the period 1760–1850 were situated in these four regions. In 1831, the two counties of Lancashire and the West Riding alone possessed a stunning 55% of all manufacturing employment in the United Kingdom demonstrating the revolutionary character of their industrial growth.[6]

DEMOGRAPHICS

This growth took place in tandem with a rapid expansion of the British population from approximately 6.3 million in 1761 to 14.9 million in 1841. This expansion was most rapid from 1791 to 1831. Such growth is particularly impressive given the heavy emigration from Britain to the colonies and to the United States as well as the long years of war that punctuated this era. Declining mortality played an important role, particularly among infants and young children, but increasing fertility was a greater factor in the impressive increase in British population. Increased fertility resulted from several factors. The mean age of marriage fell from 28 for males and 26 for females in the decade 1680–1689 to 25 for men and 23 for women in 1830–1837. Women increasingly expected to marry. Married women were also slightly more likely to have children and to minimize the spacing between births. These shifts in nuptiality were an essential component of the increased fertility of the period.

URBANIZATION

Not only was the population growing, but the people were also moving to urban areas. The proportion of urban dwellers more than doubled from 21% in 1750 to 45% a century later. Increased urbanization preceded industrialization, but accelerated once the revolution was on. The urbanization of Great Britain far outpaced that of other European countries in the eighteenth century, marking the unique nature of the transformation under way in the British Isles.[7]

HOW PEOPLE LIVED—THE STANDARD OF LIVING

STANDARD OF LIVING

How did these revolutionary changes affect the standard of living? This question rises whenever impressive output growth is accompanied by a burgeoning population. Because few industries grew as fast as cotton textiles, metallurgy, or even woolens, Britain as a whole actually experienced relatively slow growth, punctuated by periodic crises.

As a result of these factors, living standards rose gradually and tentatively in the heyday of industrialization. From 1780 to 1851, the standard of living rose, at most, by 30%. Since this improvement followed a period of falling wages in the first decades of industrialization (1760–1780), industrialization did not seem to have improved British living standards—especially for the burgeoning working classes—as much or as rapidly as had been thought. Most gains did not begin to appear until 1830 or 1840, demonstrating the sacrifices that the industrial revolution imposed on the average household economy.[8]

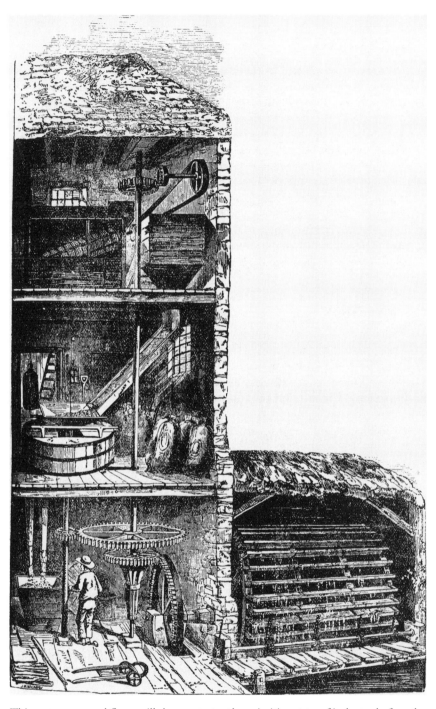

This water-powered flour mill demonstrates the primitive state of industry before the industrial revolution and the scope of the changes to come. The Burndy Library, Cambridge, Massachusetts

REAL WAGES

Shifts in the standard of living start with a discussion of real wages. Real wages increased only 16% from 1760 to 1820, an increase that is distorted by the decline of average real family incomes by approximately 14% from 1791–1795 to 1816–1820. From that point, real wages improved a dramatic 41% from 1820 to 1850. These increased real wages were partially the result of a vastly extended workweek. Without formal vacations, in 1760, an average employed British adult labored nearly 50 hours a week. By 1850, when nearly half of British workers labored in mines, mills, workshops, and factories, that figure had climbed to more than 61 hours a week. Women and children had to work outside the home to keep body and soul together. Pushed by declining hourly wages and increasing hours of labor for men, perhaps two-thirds of married women earned wages or had an occupation in the late eighteenth century. In 1851, census data indicates that 36% of children aged 10–14 worked. Thanks to all these hands and the increased hours worked by men, consumption was able to increase about 75% in 1750–1850. People also bought different things (see Chapters 2 and 8). Nonessential spending (on goods other than food and lodging) increased 137% between 1789–1796 and 1830–1839 while household budgets increased only 43%, in large part because of declining prices, particularly for clothes and other consumer products.

Other measures tell a similarly ambivalent story. The height of army recruits—a unique source that provides insight into nutrition and health conditions—declined by 1.3%. In 1850, the average British male was probably shorter than he had been a century before. Continental Europe did not experience a similar drop. Such data might be explained in part by increased consumption of sugar, tobacco, and alcohol by the average consumer. British life expectancy at birth had stood at 42.7 years in 1581, but fell rapidly until it reached a mere 25.3 years in 1726! By 1826, it was back to 41.3 years before declining to 39.5 years in 1850. Of course, some groups enjoyed consistently longer lives, but as a whole, mid-Victorian British life expectancy was less than it had been under Queen Elizabeth.[9]

ROBERT OWEN

The magnitude and rapidity of the changes associated with the industrial revolution were evident to discerning contemporaries. Robert Owen (1771–1858), a Welsh factory manager in Manchester, struck out on his own in 1800 to establish the first of four large cotton mills at New Lanark, Scotland. He was a social reformer who founded schools and reduced the length of the workday in his mills from 13–14 hours to 10 and a half. He published an essay entitled "Observations on the Effect of the Manufacturing System" in 1815 that was intended to persuade Parliament to limit the exploitation of child labor in the factories: some of his reform proposals were enacted in the Factory Act of 1819. His more humane approach to management earned the enterprise consistently large profits. During the 29 years he directed the mills, he more than doubled the capital of the investors. In later life, Owen's critique of industrial society led him to embrace utopian socialism as a means of preserving the egalitarian and communal lifestyles of the rural population.

From the first, Owen recognized the importance of the changes of the industrial revolution for a large segment of society. He stated that, "Those who were engaged in the trade, manufactures, and commerce of this country thirty or forty years ago formed but a very insignificant portion of the knowledge, wealth, influence or population of the Empire."[10] But that by 1815, "nearly half as many more persons are engaged in trade as in agriculture." Technological innovation in the cotton industry "caused an extraordinary demand for almost all the manufactures previously established, and, of course, for human labour."

Owen was vitally concerned with the effects of industrialization on British national character.

The general diffusion of manufactures throughout a country generates a new character in its inhabitants; and as this character is formed upon a principle quite unfavourable to individual or general happiness, it will produce the most lamentable and permanent evils, unless its tendency be counteracted by legislative interference and direction.

The manufacturing system has already so far extended its influence over the British Empire, as to effect an essential change in the general character of the mass of the people. This alteration is still in rapid progress; and ere long, the comparatively happy simplicity of the agricultural peasant will be wholly lost amongst us. . .

The acquisition of wealth, and the desire which it naturally creates for a continued increase, have introduced a fondness for essentially injurious luxuries among a numerous class of individuals who formerly never thought of them, and they have also generated a disposition which strongly impels its possessors to sacrifice the best feelings of human nature to this love of accumulation.

For Owen, this "love of accumulation" on the part of workers soon became "oppression" as wages fell. He found that "[i]n the manufacturing districts it is common for parents to send their children of both sexes at seven or eight years of age" into the factories from 6 A.M. to 8 P.M.: "children now find they must labour incessantly for their bare subsistence." Owen believed that this situation was the "overwhelming effect of the system under which they have been trained." Industrialization was necessary to provide employment for the rapidly growing population and to generate wealth, but, in the eyes of this sympathetic entrepreneur at least, the cultural changes that accompanied the initial stages of industrialization were understood to be a two-edged sword that rent the fabric of society. This sort of ambivalence on the part of entrepreneurs, workers, and bureaucrats is an essential part of the industrial revolution that is missing from most contemporary accounts, but will be woven into the story told in succeeding chapters.

2

THE BUILDING BLOCKS
OF A NEW ECONOMY

IDEAS, AIMS, AND METHODS

ENLIGHTENMENT

What made the industrial revolution possible was the dawn of a new way of thinking—this fundamental shift is known as the Enlightenment. Curiosity was the watchword of the Enlightenment; the investigations and explorations it spawned led not only to a different conception of the universe, but also shifted perceptions of what humans could accomplish. As a social movement, the Enlightenment emerged in the late seventeenth century as a means of criticizing two dominant institutions: the Roman Catholic Church and the absolutist French monarchy under Louis XIV (1638–1715). Thanks to the Scientific Revolution of the sixteenth and seventeenth centuries, which pioneered a great transformation in how educated Europeans conceived of the natural world, the Enlightenment was able to investigate new areas of inquiry and to spread existing knowledge more widely than ever. The purpose of these actions was to undermine the pretensions of either church or state to exclusive and universal knowledge. The men and women who contributed to the Enlightenment were not content with these successes; they set even more far-reaching goals. To improve the human condition, these people focused on understanding and controlling the natural environment. This project of improvement through understanding lay the foundations for greater interaction between science and technology. In the nineteenth century, this linkage would become important to the continuation of industrial growth after the onset of the industrial revolution.

NEWTON

The Enlightenment drew crucial support for its attack on exclusive claims to knowledge from the breakthroughs of an Englishman, Isaac Newton

(1643–1727). Newton and German Gottfried Liebniz (1646–1716) earned the disdain of generations of students by simultaneously developing calculus, a branch of mathematics that was an essential tool to explaining the physics of the universe. In his major work, published in 1687, Newton reconfigured European understandings of celestial mechanics (the movement of heavenly bodies) and explained his three laws of motion. For those with the mathematical skills to decipher the formulas—not to mention the ungrammatical Latin Newton wrote in—this work definitively obliterated the dominant religious and scientific conceptions of the universe almost uniformly based on Aristotle. Newton's explanation of the universe was convincing to the scientific community until the breakthroughs of Albert Einstein and Werner Heisenberg in the first half of the twentieth century. These stunning achievements were not enough for Newton. He also made important discoveries in optics, which led to new theories concerning the properties of light and colors that culminated in the invention of the reflecting telescope. Despite the efforts of gifted writers such as John Locke and Voltaire, who published popular and popularized explanations of Newton's ideas in 1704 and 1733 respectively, it took decades for Newton's ideas to percolate through the educated strata of Western society. Such fundamental conceptual reordering of the understanding of the universe demonstrated the possibilities of human endeavor and took the prestige of English science and technology to new heights.

ENCYCLOPÉDIE

Following up the insights of the Scientific Revolution, the eighteenth century was marked by the diffusion of ideas. Frenchmen Denis Diderot (1713–1784) and Jean le Rond d'Alembert (1717–1783) led a great collaborative enterprise. To rationalize and categorize existing knowledge, they published a twenty-four-volume compendium of existing knowledge, the *Encyclopédie*, between 1751 and 1772. Diderot and d'Alembert had to overcome the opposition of powerful individuals in the Church hierarchy and state administration. Other eighteenth-century projects of diffusion and rationalization included the creation of the periodic table of elements and Swede Carl von Linné's (or Linnaeus 1707–1778) development of a means of classifying plants and animals into categories. The organization and publication of current scientific knowledge set the stage for greater accomplishments to follow.

A NEW METHODOLOGY

Although science made few direct contributions to manufacturing technology during the first few decades of the industrial revolution, it did accomplish something vital. The Scientific Revolution bequeathed a new inductive method of testing ideas that focused on experimentation. The wave of scientific discoveries, clever experiments, and geographical explorations that followed helped to convince the average person that an improvement of the human condition was possible. The prospect of "progress," both in understanding and materially, gradually overcame the pessimistic views of people like Thomas Malthus that had dominated European society for a millennium. In the nineteenth century, this faith in progress became concrete as technological change and industrialization first transformed the day to day life of western Europeans, and ultimately, much of the world.

AGRICULTURAL TRANSFORMATION

AGRICULTURAL REVOLUTION

Perhaps the most important precondition for the industrial revolution was a revolution in agriculture. This revolution occurred in technique, not in technology. The methods employed to increase crop yields had been known for centuries, but only came into widespread use in western Europe in the seventeenth and eighteenth centuries. Particularly in Great Britain, the Dutch Republic and parts of northern France, the timing of implementation stemmed from population pressure and elite desires for greater profits from their landholdings. Commercial agriculture replaced subsistence farming thanks to a host of factors that included: irrigation; greater use of draft animals; different crop rotations that included grasses and clover to permit land to recover from growing grain that also provided fodder to feed larger herds of animals; more thorough breeding of animals; the systematic use of fertilizer; the enclosure of common land; the consolidation of plots; and the clearing of new land. These improvements helped to create larger farms, maximized the income of landowners, allowed a significant number of people to eat better, and increased the available quantity of agricultural commodities.

The Agricultural Revolution had dramatic economic consequences. The production of more grain permitted urban areas to grow. Improved techniques meant that less labor was needed for agriculture: a greater percentage of the population could now labor in industry. By increasing yields, farmers made more money, which enabled them to purchase manufactured goods. The production of more food allowed prices to fall despite the increasing population. Declining food prices also meant that people could eat more: the decline in the number of stillborn children and in infant mortality is powerful evidence of improved nutrition. Escalating landlord profits that were generated by commercial agriculture could be invested in industry. In short, without the capital and other improvements provided by the agricultural revolution, the industrial revolution would not have taken place when or where it did. The agricultural revolution affected the daily lives of far, far more people than the early stages of industrialization.

Most of the gains from the agricultural revolution were realized by 1750. It preceded and permitted the onset of industrialization. *During* the industrial revolution, although total output and labor productivity continued to improve, the increments were far less than in the period from 1600 to 1750. Much of the growth in output was derived by increasing the land in cultivation. Nor did agriculture provide a vital market for manufactures, generate new capital, or release labor. The finding that the benefits of agricultural transformation did not continue during the industrial revolution is the result of recent research; its importance stems firstly from the fact that it shows a continuous process of economic transformation operating in northwestern Europe beginning in the seventeenth century and secondly because it refocuses attention on demand rather than supply as a cause for the emergence of the industrial revolution.

The Enlightenment shaped agricultural improvement. Arthur Young (1741–1820), a leading English agricultural writer, emphasized the importance of education, the development of new knowledge, and the utility of helping agricultural entrepreneurs to escape the binding restrictions of customary practice through innovation.

What a gross absurdity, to bind down in the fetters of custom ten intelligent men willing to adopt the improvements adapted to enclosures, because one stupid fellow is obstinate for the practice of his grandfather! To give ignorance the power to limit knowledge, to render stupidity the measure of talents, to chain down industry to the non-exertions of indolence, and fix an insuperable bar, a perpetual exclusion, to all that energy of improvement which has carried husbandry to perfection by means of enclosure![1]

He also connected the desire to improve agriculture to the desire for increased profits and noted how important that desire was for the good of the entire nation:

By giving an exclusive property to the soil, the proprietor has his industry unfettered; he is allowed to expend his capital; he is permitted to apply his lands to whatever use will pay him best; he neither burdens his neighbour, nor is shackled by him: no barbarous customs prohibit his exertions: his talents, his energy and capital, are free to be employed for his own benefit; he thrives, and national prosperity follows in his train.[2]

As the statistics reveal concretely, Young's fervor for agricultural improvement was shared by an impressive number of other people in Great Britain (see insert).

François de Quesnay (1694–1774)

Quesnay was an important French economic thinker in the age of Enlightenment. A group of like-minded individuals adopted many of his ideas: this group came to be known as the Physiocrats. His ideas reached a wide audience through Diderot and d'Alembert's *Encyclopédie* in which the following excerpt appeared in 1756. This passage demonstrates the central importance of farming to social prosperity as Quesnay and his followers attempted to apply the lessons of agricultural revolution to France. He also stresses the entrepreneurial skills needed by successful agricultural innovators.

> Yet it is evident that the only means available to the government to make commerce flourish and to sustain and extend industry is to achieve an increase of revenues; because these revenues alone call into being the merchants and artisans and pay for their services. It is necessary, then, to cultivate the base of the tree and not to limit oneself to trimming the branches; let us leave them to arrange themselves and to spread freely; but let us not neglect the land which furnishes the necessary sap for their nourishment and growth.... The lands cultivated in plots by small farmer demand more men and expense and the profits are much more limited. Now, men and expenditures must not be wasted in works which could be more profitable to the state if executed with fewer men and less expense. This bad use of men for cultivation of the land would be prejudicial even in a highly populated kingdom; because the more it is populated, the more necessary it is to derive a large return from the land ... The advantages of agriculture depend heavily then, on combining lands into larger farms, put in the best state of cultivation by rich farmers ... We do not envisage the rich farmer as a worker who himself works the land; he is an entrepreneur who directs and gives value to his enterprise by his intelligence and wealth. Agriculture carried on by rich cultivators is a very honest and lucrative profession, reserved to free men able to advance the considerable sums that the cultivation of the land demands that occupies the peasants and always provides them with a generous and assured profit.

Source: François de Quesnay, "Grain," in the *Encyclopédia* (1756), cited in John Bowditch and Clement Ramsland, eds., *Voices of the Industrial Revolution: Selected Readings from the Liberal Economists and Their Critics* (Ann Arbor: University of Michigan Press, 1957), 9–10.

CONSUMERS AND THEIR ACTIONS

INDUSTRIOUS REVOLUTION

Both the Enlightenment and the Agricultural Revolution were intimately linked to another major shift in how people lived and worked during this period. Simply put, in the seventeenth and eighteenth centuries, an increasing number of people linked together in family units worked harder and longer not only to keep body and soul together, but increasingly to get things they wanted for their own use or consumption. This intensification of human endeavor has been termed the "industrious revolution" by Jan DeVries. He

With this kind of loom, women engaged in industrial labor in the home while men performed other tasks. The Burndy Library, Cambridge, Massachusetts

argues that households "made decisions that increased *both* the supply of marketed commodities and labor *and* the demand for goods offered in the marketplace." Two factors made this possible: a reduction of leisure time—on the part of men, women, and children—in favor of wage labor; and a shift from producing a wide variety of goods and services for direct consumption to purchasing marketed goods.

This latter switch implied greater specialization and helped to increase productivity. This process was independent of the organizational and technological developments associated with the industrial revolution.[3]

CONSUMER REVOLUTION

What caused this willingness to work harder and longer? Both contemporaries and historians point to the emergence of a seemingly insatiable consumer demand for luxury goods and colonial commodities that affected most of northwestern Europe. Although the passion for fashion was noticeable–mostly among the elite and the growing middle classes–the demand for new consumer goods also extended to the laboring classes. It was so widespread and so significant a shift that it has been termed the "consumer revolution."[4] There was, however, an important division between the upper and middle classes whose interest in the new, the fashionable, and in taste extended to all categories of available goods, and the lower classes who focused more on

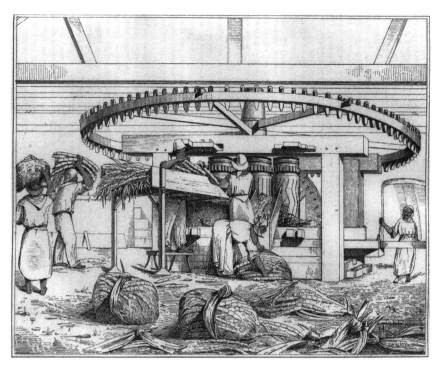

Sugar production was an industrial as well as an agricultural process. This mill crushed the cane before it was distilled into gin. Slaves handled all parts of the job with minimal supervision. The Burndy Library, Cambridge, Massachusetts

commodities they could *consume*. These goods included tea, coffee, chocolate, tobacco, and sugar, but beer and spirits were also consumed in increasing quantities. The addictive properties of these commodities made many laboring families willing to work longer and harder to get their cup of tea, chocolate fix or tobacco product of choice[5] (see Chapter 8). As the Scottish economist James Stueart put it in 1767: "Men are forced to labour now because they are slaves to their own wants."[6]

Thus, as with the agricultural revolution, both an industrious revolution and a consumer revolution predated the onset of revolutionary industrial transformation. The similarity of these preconditions once again demonstrates the central importance of demand in calling forth innovative organizational and technological means of meeting potent consumer demand.

TRANSPORT

COMMERCIAL REVOLUTION

Underlying these developments was yet another "revolution": the commercial. But this revolution [see below] would have been impossible without

Adam Smith (1723–1790)

Born in Scotland, Smith studied at Glasgow University and then Oxford before becoming a professor at Glasgow in 1751. In later life, Smith was a customs commissioner until appointed lord rector of the University of Glasgow in 1787. He was deeply committed to the Enlightenment, not only in Great Britain where he was a close friend of David Hume and had ties to Samuel Johnson, Edward Gibbon, and Benjamin Franklin, but also in France where he met Voltaire and d'Alembert. He was also in dialogue with François Quesnay and Anne-Robert-Jacques Turgot. Although considered the founder of economics as a scientific discipline, *An Inquiry into the Nature and Causes of the Wealth of Nations* published in 1776 reveals Smith's actual expertise in moral philosophy. This work was originally delivered as a series of lectures at Glasgow. He discussed the pros and cons of the division of labor, the importance of caring for the laboring classes, and the nature of the invisible hand, that is, how individual self-interest tends to benefit all through the mechanism of an unfettered market. Despite his support for "laissez-faire," this term has been misunderstood. It means "enough to do" rather than "hands off" which is evident in how Smith identified important areas of state action that limited individual choices and the supposed free play of the market. Many commentators have misunderstood how extensive the areas covered by these three duties of the state are and how important they are to Smith's understanding of the proper functioning of a society.

> According to the system of natural liberty, the sovereign has only three duties to attend to; three duties of great importance, indeed, but plain and intelligible to common understandings: first, the duty of protecting the society from the violence and invasion of other independent societies; secondly, the duty of protecting, as far as possible, every member of the society form the injustice or oppression of every other member of it, or the duty of establishing an exact administration of justice; and, thirdly, the duty of erecting and maintaining public works and certain public institutions . . . [Book IV, Chapter 9]

> When the institutions or public works which are beneficial to the whole society, either cannot be maintained altogether, or are not maintained altogether by the contribution of such particular members of the society as are most immediately benefited by them, the deficiency must in most cases be made up by the general contribution of the whole society. The general revenue of the society, over and above defraying the expense of defending the society, and of supporting the dignity of the chief magistrate, must make up for the deficiency of many particular branches of revenue. [Book V, Chapter 1]*

*Edwin Cannan, ed., *Adam Smith: The Wealth of Nations* (New York: The Modern Library, 2000), 745, 878.

improvements to the British transportation network. Two intertwined developments were especially important. Internal transportation (within a state's boundaries) was vastly improved in the seventeenth and eighteenth centuries and then again in the nineteenth. In the eighteenth century, water transport was significantly less expensive than overland. Adam Smith (see insert) described the situation:

A broad-wheeled waggon, attended by two men, and drawn by eight horses, in about six weeks time carries and brings back between London and Edinburgh near four ton weight of goods. In about the same time a ship navigated by six or eight men, and sailing between the ports of London and Leith, frequently carries and brings back two hundred ton weight of goods. Six or eight men, therefore, by the help of water-carriage, can carry and bring back in the same time the same quantity of goods between London and Edinburgh, as fifty broad-wheeled waggons, attended by a hundred men, and drawn by four hundred horses.[7]

At the dawn of the eighteenth century, road transport costs averaged about 1 shilling per ton-mile while shipping via inland waterways cost about 2.5 pence per mile and coastal shipping even less.[8] This difference of at least 480% in shipping costs demonstrates the extreme expense of transporting heavy or bulky goods by land.

CANALS

The differential in shipping costs encouraged greater investment and innovation. Cheap coal was so critical to the British economy that canals were built to transport it to market. Beginning around 1750, canals were constructed along the Severn, Trent, and Mersey Rivers and their tributaries. Later, canals linked the river systems or facilitated access to inland areas like southern Wales that had vital resources but no outlet to the sea (see insert). With the exception of the canal constructed by the Duke of Bridgewater to link his estates to Manchester and Liverpool, the construction of most canals was financed through joint-stock companies to mobilize the enormous sums needed. By 1830, England and Wales had 3,876 miles of inland canals, up from 1,399 in 1760.[9] From 1780 to 1830, canals contributed a 0.8% annual increase in transport productivity.[10]

WATER TRANSPORT

Harbors and rivers were dredged and deepened to permit additional or further access. Even before the use of steam revolutionized ocean transport, sailing ships were modified through different rigging and hull design to increase carrying capacity while lessening the number of men needed to work a vessel. On ships entering London from Spain and Portugal, the size of the vessel grew rapidly: the number of tons per man increased from 7.9 in 1686 to 9.1 in 1726 to 12.6 in 1766.[11] Shipping contributed a 1.4% annual increase in transport productivity between 1780 and 1860.[12] Such gradual improvements helped to develop England's transportation network to a level

Francis Egerton (1736–1803), Third Duke of Bridgewater

As a 17-year-old, Egerton embarked on the Grand Tour of the European continent that many noble Englishmen took to complete their educations. While on tour, he visited the Canal du Midi in France that linked the Atlantic and Mediterranean Seas. Inspired by this great engineering feat as well as by the St. Helens Canal that brought coal to the Mersey River, which emptied at Liverpool, in 1758, Egerton determined to construct a canal. He hoped to profit more from the output of the extensive coal deposits at his estate at Worsley. The investment was worth it because of the staggering 9–10 shillings a ton cost of transporting coal the seven miles to Manchester. This cost priced Worsley coal out of the market. After consulting two noted engineers: James Gilbert who drew up the plans and James Brindley who oversaw construction—the decision was taken to solve the mine's drainage problems while allowing for more profitable exploitation of the mine by building a canal to the edge of Manchester.

The technical difficulties involved were enormous. The directors of an existing canal, the Mersey & Irwell, made them worse by obstructing the project. The difficulties to be surmounted included the need to construct a significant portion of the canal underground; another was how to cross the Mersey & Irwell. The answer was to build an aqueduct 38 feet above the existing canal. Needless to say, this proposal was widely ridiculed by contemporaries. Despite the staggering cost of about "10,000 guineas [each worth 21 shillings or 1.05 pounds] a mile," the section of the canal running from Worsley to Castlefield in Manchester was completed in 1761. The canal boats were drawn by horses until the late nineteenth century. Once Worsley coal began to reach Manchester by water, the price of coal in the city fell by half. John Philips, the well-known author of *A Treatise on Inland Navigation* published in 1785 commented that, "This mine had lain dormant in the bowels of the hearth from time immemorial without the least profit to the noble owner, on account of the price of land carriage which was so excessive that they could not be sold at a reasonable price."

In 1762, Egerton embarked on a major expansion of the canal to link Manchester and Liverpool. It took more than a decade to complete this section because the marshy ground was hard to stabilize. Ultimately about 47 miles of underground canal were constructed at four different levels as links between Egerton's canals. Other waterways were constructed to form a network. Building these additions nearly bankrupted Egerton, but, by the end of the century, he had recouped his investment and begun to make substantial profits. Known as the "Canal Duke," Egerton was an enthusiastic supporter of canals and canal-building throughout his adult life. His heirs sold the canal network in the 1870s for a huge profit and the canals remained in commercial operation until 1974.

Sources: Paul Mantoux, *The Industrial Revolution in the Eighteenth Century: An Outline of the Beginnings of the Modern Factory System in England* (New York: Harper & Row, 1961), 123–25. The quotations were reproduced in Mathias, *The First Industrial Nation*, 98, 105.

beyond those of their European competitors and set the stage for further improvements once steam power was added to the mix.

ROADS

Roads were also attended to in the seventeenth and eighteenth centuries. They needed it. Britain's roads were in sorrowful shape. The growth of London encouraged local entrepreneurs in the provinces to improve and maintain the roads leading to the capital. These activities were paid for by charging tolls. Beginning in the mid-seventeenth century, but accelerating rapidly after 1750, these turnpikes were developed into a national network. By 1770, they effectively tied the island together.

Turnpikes and other toll roads made use of important developments in road-building. Roads were strengthened by tightly packing them with small stones. Drainage was improved by fashioning convex surfaces. As early as 1828, concrete was applied to roads. Many more tunnels and bridges were also built thereby avoiding dangerous conditions or lengthy detours. The turnpikes shortened travel time especially for passengers and the mail. Going the 413 miles from London to Edinburgh took 10–12 days in the 1750s, but, by the 1830s, it was advertised to be a mere "42 hours, 33 minutes!"[13] A rapidly expanding network set of coach services both for freight and for passengers took advantage of the improving road system. Competition among a multitude of private companies hastened a fall in prices of perhaps one-third while encouraging service improvements. By the mid-1830s, 22,000 miles of roads had either been turnpiked or were administered by professionals; this represented one-fifth of all roads on the island.[14] Roads witnessed a 0.7% annual growth in transport productivity between 1690 and 1840.[15]

EFFECTS OF TRANSPORT IMPROVEMENT

These improvements in transportation had myriad effects. Important technical innovations were developed: in road- and ship-building; in hull and coach design; in dredging and river management; in the creation of new material mixes for constructing roads; and in the building of locks and sluices, among other things. Engineers of all types and the construction industries in general benefited directly from the development of the transportation net. British financial practice evolved to raise the sums needed to improve the roads, waterways, and shipping. Various organizations within British society learned to work together to link up the disparate parts of the network. Developing the technical expertise of Britain's human capital, mobilizing finance capital and evolving forms of organization contributed appreciably to the emergence of industrial society in the late eighteenth century.

The economic implications of the improvements in transportation were dramatic. Despite the piecemeal character of road and canal building, with no national planning either attempted or implemented, an island-spanning network was created, linking the major urban centers together and reaching out into most rural areas. Food prices fell, not by reducing the incomes of those who worked the land, but by lowering market prices. Most commodity prices also dropped, especially that of coal. The economic benefits of an improved transportation network even before the steamboat and the railroad were so clear that entrepreneurs relocated production to take advantage of natural resources, especially if coal was available nearby. All in all, roads, canals, and shipping permitted first the development and then the integration of British markets by substantially lowering transaction costs.

A GLOBAL ECONOMY: TRADE, COLONIALISM, AND EMPIRE

TRADE

Internal transportation was complemented by broader developments to create a commercial revolution. The two key processes at work were the opening up of the western hemisphere or "New World" and the emergence of an Atlantic economic system. The bulk of British overseas trade was with other European countries, but over the course of the seventeenth and eighteenth centuries, a burgeoning complementary interchange developed with other parts of the Atlantic world. This trade was supplemented by growing commerce with Asia, particularly India and China. As we shall see, the growth of British foreign trade and its part in the "commercial revolution" was linked intimately to the development of its Empire.

TRADE WITH ASIA

It was trade in "oriental" goods: spices, especially pepper; cotton and silk textiles; tea; and coffee that began the "take off" of British long-distance trade. European demand for these goods was exceptionally strong, but was not matched by an equivalent Asian desire for European products. Europeans had to pay for the pepper, cottons, and silks with hard money—gold and silver—that they did not have. The specie that underlay European trade with Asia came overwhelmingly from the Americas. Spain and Portugal began to conquer and colonize the "New World" early in the sixteenth century initiating huge transfers of bullion, first by expropriation and then from mining. A century later, the development of plantations by a host of European states grew tropical and semitropical commodities such as tobacco, then sugar, cotton, chocolate, coffee, and rice. The plantations furthered the development of an economy focused on furnishing raw materials to Europe either for its own consumption or to pass along to Asia. The labor demands of mining and plantation agriculture spurred the rapid increase in the acquisition of millions of human slaves from Africa. Thus, two trade triangles emerged. First, gold and silver from the Americas to Asia passed through European intermediaries in exchange for "oriental" goods that were consumed in Europe. Second, man-ufactured goods were sent from Europe or re-exported from Asia to Africa where they were exchanged for human beings who were then brought to the Americas to mine precious metals for trade with Asia and grow agricultural commodities for consumption in Europe.

INDUSTRIALIZATION AND COLONIZATION

A convincing recent exploration of trade patterns by Joseph Inikori empha-sizes the dependence of Europeans on the exploitation of Africans—whether those who remained at home or those who were taken away to become slaves in the Americas—to furnish the goods and precious metals necessary to trade with Asia and that generated the markets and capital that underpinned the industrial revolution. This interpretation focuses attention on the relationship of exploitation to the emergence of industrial society, not just within Europe, but around the world. Kenneth Pomeranz's provocative comparison of China and Europe complements Inikori's findings. Pomeranz contends that what enabled Europe to industrialize first rather than China was privileged access to the resources and markets of the Americas. Thus, the emergence of the Atlantic economy was of world historical significance.

What is most striking about these developments, however, is that this enormously profitable Atlantic economy emerged alongside significant con-tinued growth of European trade with Asia and within Europe. These various commercial networks created a true global economy as more and more ar-eas were incorporated into a world trading system with Europe as the hub. Taken together these developments were the foundation of the "commercial revolution."

COLONIALISM

The British played an important and growing role in the development of these trade networks. Colonialism was essential to this process. From the sixteenth century, English access to the wealth of Asia and the Americas was blocked by the Spanish and the Portuguese. The Dutch, English, and French fought the putative monopoly of the Iberian powers both by direct conquest of Spanish and Portuguese trading stations, forts, and settlements and by founding their own communities in unoccupied areas to create their own spheres of influence. Colonial conquest and commercial exploitation rapidly became a free-for-all in which all powers preyed on each other as well as on native populations. This activity was part of a series of wars fought by European powers all over the globe that lasted more than 125 years. Through conquest and colonization, Britain acquired most of the eastern half continent of North America, a host of possessions in the Caribbean led by Jamaica, trading stations on the coast of Africa and scattered outposts on the subcontinent of India among other territories and spheres of interest spread out across the globe.

ATLANTIC TRADE

Colonies were the foundation of the global trading network operated by Great Britain. At the heart of this system was the growth of the Atlantic economy:

Annual Average Value of Atlantic Commerce (Exports, Re-exports, Imports, and Services)[16]

1651–1670	£20,084,000
1711–1760	£35,638,000
1761–1780	£57,696,000
1781–1800	£105,546,000
1848–1850	£231,046,000

Source: Inikori, *Africans and the Industrial Revolution*, 202.

African labor, both in Africa and in the Americas, generated the wealth that financed the bulk of this burgeoning trade. Exports made up a little less than 40% of these totals. Of those totals, Inikori estimated that Africans produced no less than 69% in 1651–1670 and in 1848–1850 and up to 83% in 1761–1780.[17] For Britain, whose economy made up about one-third of the Atlantic total, the rate of increase in Atlantic trade was far superior to that for other regions. Whereas total British foreign trade doubled over the course of the eighteenth century, British Atlantic trade increased by a factor of twelve in that same period![18]

The expansion of trade on this scale had a multitude of effects. British manufactured products were sold in protected markets long before their competitive advantage emerged. Commercial expansion spurred the development and application of new technologies. The wide range of territories that became tied into this global trading network required different trading goods, thereby promoting commercial and industrial diversification. In addition, the size of the domestic market no longer determined the scale of potential demand, a factor that was of critical importance in newly emerging sectors like cotton textiles.

Huge profits were made that could be reinvested. Different forms of business practice such as joint-stock companies and commercial institutions like stock markets had to be created to deal with the enormous capital invested. New, exciting, and sometimes addictive products were now available to many more Europeans which encouraged and, in some cases, forced them to work harder and for longer hours to get their "fix." Britain's merchant fleet grew spectacularly to deal with the expansion of trade. From a total tonnage of 323,000 in 1700, the merchant marine reached over a million tons in 1788.[19] The British state also received large tax revenues that amounted to a quarter of its revenues. In short, the Commercial Revolution based in the Atlantic was the means by which Britain developed the legal, financial, and commercial institutions and expertise that supported the industrial revolution that followed on its heels.

MERCANTILISM AND DOMESTIC INDUSTRY

MERCANTILISM

All early modern governments attempted to improve the economy of their states. This goal has been associated with the policy of mercantilism that attempted to increase exports in order to create a favorable balance of trade while maximizing the supply of precious metals. This approach conflated hard money and national wealth. Mercantilist policies focused on foreign trade, but a variety of institutions such as the guilds favored both low cost *and* luxury producers who could capture and keep markets abroad. States sought to garner exclusive trading privileges through treaties and all colonies were exploited to benefit the mother country. Consumers thus suffered in favor of producers. Mercantilism was practiced by all early modern European states to a greater or lesser degree, but nowhere was mercantilism more imbricated into the political culture than in Great Britain.

DOMESTIC INDUSTRY

The conservation of domestic markets and resources was at the heart of mercantilism. In this era, overall commercial self-sufficiency required increasing the production of trade goods, most notably textiles. Because the guilds were unwilling or unable to produce the kinds, qualities, and quantities of goods demanded by other continents as well as by the burgeoning European population, other methods of satisfying these markets had to be developed. To sidestep guild restrictions on urban production, entrepreneurs, including merchants, nobles, and even state officials initiated a production process that came to be known as the "putting out" system or "domestic industry." Raw materials were provided by an entrepreneur to a family that undertook the spinning and/or weaving of first wool or linen and then cotton. The raw materials were "put out" either on commission, or more commonly sold to the family. Upon completion, it was collected by or resold to the entrepreneur and then sold yet again to an urban merchant who took charge of the fabric for its ultimate retail market. The resulting profits could then be used to restart the production cycle.

THE IMPACT OF POVERTY

Many rural families engaged in "domestic industry" because the effects of population growth outstripped the gains of the agricultural revolution, at least in the short term. Put another way, there were too many people trying to survive by working too little land. Rural overpopulation forced farming families to do additional labor to survive if they wanted to remain on the land. For many families, domestic industry filled the slack winter months when there were relatively few agricultural tasks to perform. It was a supplement rather than a replacement for full-time agricultural work. In 1751, a French inspector of manufacturing reported that a weaver "buys the thread for the cloth that he wants to make. If he can sell it, he can eat and spend in proportion to the profit. When there is no demand, he has no other resources. If the situation continues, he must beg for food."[20]

In other families, women and children devoted their efforts to industry while males worked either on their own farm or for others. Only in a few places was domestic industry a full-time, year-round occupation. Some liked the ability to work on their own schedule, enjoying a few days off for a festival following the completion of an order. In general, spinning was women's work and weaving was a male pursuit; children helped out wherever they were needed. British industrialist and pamphleteer Andrew Ure observed that "The workshop of the weaver was a rural cottage ... The cotton wool which was to form his weft was picked clean by the fingers of his younger children, and was carded and spun by the older girls assisted by his wife, and the yarn was woven by himself assisted by his sons ... One good weaver could keep three active women at work upon the wheel, spinning weft."[21]

The "putting-out" system had tremendous productive potential and played a major role in accelerating the interaction of the rural populace with local, national, and international markets. A prosperous shopkeeper or affluent farmer required only a limited amount of capital to begin finding client families. The profitability of the system was based on the low wages given to the rural workers, who accepted a pittance because they needed only to supplement their agricultural income. Rural wages were at least 20% and up to 50% lower than their urban equivalents.[22] Yet careful and thrifty workers could better themselves. In Rouen, capital of Normandy, the center of French industry, an official described a female spinner's entrepreneurialism:

If she has only enough money to pay for three pounds of raw cotton, she buys no more. She works with this small amount, and works with care. When the cotton is spun she sells it that much more advantageously as her work is perfect. From the proceeds, she subtracts enough for her subsistence, and if her small capital has now increased, she buys a larger amount of raw material.[23]

Eventually, "putting out" came to dominate whole regions of Europe and contributed substantially to total industrial output. From Ireland to Prussia, dense networks of rural outworkers numbering in the hundreds of thousands and stretching up to 80 kilometers in a given direction came to surround many large mercantile cities that shipped goods abroad. In the Austrian Netherlands (modern-day Belgium), a quarter of the working population toiled in domestic industry.[24] In addition to textiles, goods that were "put out" included gloves, lace, ribbons, stockings, hats, boots, shoes, pins, nails, and cutlery, as well as other hardware. At the end of the eighteenth century, the putting-out system accounted for 43% of all German manufactured goods. By increasing textile production, spreading spinning and weaving skills to the rural population and introducing a market mentality into the day-to-day lives of many Europeans, the "putting out" system paved the way for industrialization. As a form of production, rural industry also lasted alongside the newer means of production until the 1930s.

THE ROLE OF THE STATE

MERCANTILIST POLICIES

Conserving domestic markets and resources was also behind the promulgation of a series of English Navigation Acts beginning in 1651. Intended to protect the domestic merchant marine from Dutch competition, these Acts mandated that goods from Asia, Africa, and the Americas could only be imported into Britain or its colonies in British ships. Goods from Europe either had to be carried by British ships or by ships of the origin of the goods in question. Certain colonial commodities like sugar, tea, and tobacco were required to be shipped directly to a British port even if its ultimate destination was somewhere else (this was why the proportion of re-exports was so high.) Although the British were, by far, the most successful at enforcing their Navigation Acts because of their growing maritime supremacy, nearly all European nations had similar legislation on the books in the seventeenth and eighteenth centuries.[25]

CHARTERED COMPANIES

European states all licensed associations of investors to explore, colonize, and trade with certain areas. These associations were chartered by the state which provided some support, but which left the vast majority of the activities of these associations unregulated. Chartered companies could institute laws, fight wars, make treaties (subject to state approval), and enjoyed a monopoly of trade or colonization in their area of operation. The English established chartered companies to trade with Muscovy (1555), the Levant (1581), East India (1600), and the Hudson's Bay (1670). Other charters entrusted colonization to the Virginia Company (1606) and the Massachusetts Bay Company (1629). The Netherlands established East India (1602) and West India (1621) companies, while the French established a number of such companies to trade with the Caribbean, West Africa, and in the Indian Ocean. Many other states including Denmark, Sweden, Austria, and several German lands also created chartered companies. Several of these companies, most notably the Dutch East India, the English East India, and Hudson's Bay became virtual states within states ruling vast territories with minimal government supervision (or expense!) and earning enormous profits for investors. These companies extended the European presence, tied the global economy together, and vastly expanded world trade.

CORN LAWS

Other laws regulated the import and export of food. From 1689 to 1846, the notorious English Corn Laws forbade the export of grain unless prices were extremely cheap, thanks to a bumper crop. The intent was to encourage domestic grain production by guaranteeing that a relative scarcity would keep prices high. These laws were also seen as a means of conserving currency and avoiding dependence of foreign food supplies which could be dangerous in wartime. Until 1772, additional legislation controlled internal trade in grain, meal, flour, bread, and meat. Although the state sometimes enforced lower prices in times of scarcity, in general, these regulations kept food prices above the norm for northwestern Europe and served to limit food consumption for the average Briton. The chief difference between the regulatory system embodied by the Corn Laws and similar legislation in other countries is that these restrictions lasted more than a half-century longer in Britain than they did on the continent where, beginning in 1789, the French Revolution and Napoleon swept such laws away.

WAR

War was the crucible of government intervention in the economy. Great Britain and France fought eight wars between 1688 and 1815 occupying 65 of the intervening 127 years. Britain spent a large proportion of its military budget on its navy. The navy protected the island nation from invasion, protected British trade and the Empire, and menaced enemy coastlines and colonies. A relatively small regular army was backed up by local militia. The militia were of limited value in repelling an invasion, but had significant capability to repress domestic threats or rebellion in Scotland and Ireland.

TAXES

The sheer number and scope of these wars forced the British state to tax and spend on a scale beyond that of any contemporary government.[26] In the seventeenth century, the British state collected 2–4% of national income and 6% in wartime. For the era 1689–1815, that figure jumped to 12%. The total revenue from taxes increased by a factor of seventeen, while national income merely tripled between 1670 and 1815. In 1769, a foreign observer remarked that:

the English are taxed in the morning for the soap that washes their hands; at 9 for the coffee, the tea and the sugar they use at breakfast; at noon for the starch that powders their hair; at dinner for the salt that savours their meat; in the evening for the porter [a beer] that cheers their spirits; all day long for the light that enters their windows, and at night for the candles that light them to bed.[27]

Great Britain was the most highly taxed society of the time, but other competing states like France, Spain, Prussia, and the Dutch Republic took many steps down this same path.

BORROWING

Despite this huge increase in tax revenue, Britain could not afford to fight the series of increasingly expensive world-spanning conflicts that marked the period. The English state borrowed huge sums through the London capital market. The Bank of England was created in 1694 to help the government manage and consolidate its debt and to lower the rate of interest paid by the state. After the defeat of Napoleon, interest payments on government debt amounted to 56% of the state's income. A further 31% was spent on defense. There can be no doubt that, like its chief European competitors, Great Britain under the House of Hanover was a military regime. The development of efficient and effective means of borrowing money and limiting interest charges helped Britain win wars, slow the economic gains of its rivals, gain colonies, and allow other investments to be made. The rapid expansion of the London capital market was of critical importance in Britain's ability to take advantage of its economic opportunities and ultimately to industrialize.

LAW AND ORDER

The persistent military threat magnified the security concerns of the British elite. External security anxieties were mirrored by domestic troubles that were magnified by persistently high taxes and sky-high food prices. Troops were used regularly against elements of the population in England and Scotland in circumstances ranging from the Jacobite rebellions in Scotland in 1715 and again in 1745 to hungry villagers and, urban workers or political protesters in England. With various forms of crime growing more widespread, security of person and property were also problematic up and down the social scale until the 1830s at the earliest. Elite nervousness was reflected in changes to the legal code. Although lauded for its customary protections and the persistence of common law, English law was draconian. From 50 capital crimes at the dawn of the eighteenth century, there were nearly 200 on the books a century later. Stealing sheep, cattle, or horses carried the death penalty as did taking goods from a house when the owners were present. A thief could be executed for stealing goods from a shop, workhouse, or stable worth only 5 shillings. These harsh penalties were often commuted to transportation—sending the felon to the colonies for specified periods—but to most contemporary observers, the penalty did not seem to match the crime.

STATE SUPPORT FOR ENTREPRENEURS

The British state was also increasingly willing to deploy first law and then force on behalf of the interests of entrepreneurs. The British state delegated control of wages and prices to local Justices of the Peace who tended to reject salary demands that were not linked to rising prices. The enclosure of fields was mandated by Act of Parliament and resistance to the division of the commons was overcome by force. The same process accompanied the creation of the turnpike trusts when they infringed on or replaced local interests. Labor was also controlled more thoroughly than in the past. The system of lengthy apprenticeships was maintained and strengthened and the traditional rights of skilled workers to resist the demands of their employers were steadily eroded until they were finally eliminated in 1809–1814. Combinations of workers were outlawed while combinations of entrepreneurs were encouraged. Strikes by miners and industrial workers were broken up by force whenever property was threatened. The English legal system also enforced social control in dealing with vagrancy and unemployment. Since many jobs were seasonal, a very high proportion of workers were unemployed on an annual cycle. Those who did not have a current means of support could be sent back to the parish of their birth where they were put into a workhouse, imprisoned in a house of correction, or even transported. This Poor Law, like most of the actions of the British state in the eighteenth century, maintained or even increased the servility and dependence of the lower ranks of English society. This dependence probably made labor more productive thereby contributing to economic growth, but it did little to benefit social peace.

STATE INVESTMENT

Government resources could also be used less repressively. The state was the impetus for the improvements in transportation that marked the period. Britain invested directly to improve ships, docks, harbors, and weapons. Turnpikes and canals were created or improved thanks to government-granted monopolies. The state also attracted numerous skilled workers and inventors from abroad with monetary incentives and tax breaks. For technologies or craft practices that could not be acquired in such manner, the state resorted to commissioning and/or rewarding industrial spies. From the seventeenth century, a patent law protected the inventions or improvements of innovators. In imitation of continental academies, Charles II supported the establishment of the Royal Society to explore the world of science in 1660. Although much of this sort of activity was "behind the scenes," the fundamentally mercantilist British state was an effective supporter of economic development throughout the period.

THE CONTINENT

The British differed little in their approach to economic development from their continental rivals. The Physiocrats in France, the Cameralists in Germany, and "improvers" throughout Europe all attempted similar reforms. France, for example, shared many of the problems of public order experienced by Britain and attempted to deal with them in similar fashion—through the deployment of legal repression backed by force. The most important difference was that whereas the guild system in Great Britain was wasting away by the eighteenth century, in most of continental Europe, it was alive and well and in some ways, stronger than ever. The restrictions on what could be produced, by whom, and where served to limit economic growth in favor of quality guarantees for consumers, profits for producers, and lucrative fees paid to various levels of the state. The competing claims of local governments for jurisdiction and/or tax dollars were also far less in England and Scotland which became a unified market in 1707. All continental European states sought to eliminate interior barriers to trade. The early accomplishment of a unified national market and the shunting aside of guilds gave Britain major economic advantages in the eighteenth century. Other Europeans sought to imitate these advantages with varying degrees of success.

ADAM SMITH AND MERCANTILISM

The fundamental dependence of eighteenth-century economic growth on mercantilism by the European powers especially Great Britain in the seventeenth and eighteenth centuries has been obscured by the gigantic shadow cast by the immensely influential work of Adam Smith. For far too many economists, economic historians, and politicians, Smith's well-known attack on mercantilism in favor of a more individualistic focus on industry and free trade has assumed the status of dogma. That Smith was criticizing rather than describing contemporary practice appears to have been either forgotten or deliberately overlooked. No matter how Smith has been read by his successors, it must not be forgotten that the economic preconditions for industrialization were fostered in a thoroughly exploitative, mercantilist economic system.

REVOLUTIONS

The term "revolution" has been applied to a startling number of developments taking place in the seventeenth and eighteenth centuries. The term is not being devalued: rather, its constant use demonstrates the phenomenal depth and breadth of the changes taking place in this pivotal era. Revolutions in science, agriculture, transportation, commerce, industriousness, and consumerism combined with the Enlightenment and with European colonialism to create a fundamentally different economic environment. The opportunities, marketing strategies, and means of delivering goods that an entrepreneur

Anne-Robert-Jacques de Turgot (1727–1781)

Turgot's career demonstrates the possibilities and limitations of reform in the eighteenth century. From a well-connected Norman family with official ties, Turgot was expected to join the clergy after he won honors in theology at the Sorbonne. Instead, he entered state service. In 1761, he was sent as *intendant* [chief representative of the central state] to the sleepy generality of Limoges in rural, central France. Stunned by the backwardness of this relatively remote area, for the next 13 years, Turgot set out to improve the region. His answer to the cultural isolation of the local inhabitants was broadly-based economic development. Commerce, manufacturing, and scientific agriculture would transform every aspect of people's lives. The Limousin became a model province because Turgot was able to recruit local elites to support the twin projects of Enlightenment and economic development. Influenced by the Physiocrats, Turgot rejected the idea that hoarding precious metals was economically useful. Instead, likening commerce to the circulatory system, Turgot believed that the increased circulation of goods generated wealth for the greatest number. This perspective made Turgot the enemy of privilege and of restrictions on the market in all its forms. His reputation as an Enlightened administrator and as writer on economic subjects was such that Diderot observed that, "Turgot is one of the best men in the kingdom and perhaps one of the shrewdest in every area. He will never get out of Limoges, and if does get out, I shall jump for joy for it will mean that the spirit of our ministry will have changed utterly ... in an almost miraculous fashion."*

This miracle came in 1774 when the newly crowned Louis XVI, attracted by the ideas of reform and of economic development, made Turgot his *contrôleur-général de finances* [finance minister]. Plans for reform that infringed on privilege were bitterly opposed by interest groups. In January 1776, Turgot's reforms had to be imposed by royal fiat. His Six Edicts transmuted the labor service of the French peasantry into a tax, ended the regulation of the grain trade into Paris, and abolished the guilds among other measures. By attacking so many entrenched interests, at the same time, Turgot relied on the King for support, but he was politically outmaneuvered by his enemies. He fell from power in May 1776 and his reforms were overturned. It was clear to most contemporary observers that mastering the privileged interests that dominated French society would require a more radical solution. The limitations on economic development stemming from the enduring power of privilege revealed in Turgot's rise and fall were major reasons for the outbreak of the French Revolution in 1789.

*Daniel Roche, *France in the Enlightenment*, trans. Arthur Goldhammer (Cambridge, MA: Harvard University Press, 1998 [1993]), 235–236.

Source: The quotation is from Daniel Roche, *France in the Enlightenment*, trans. Arthur Goldhammer (Cambridge, MA: Harvard University Press, 1998 [1993]), 235–36.

faced at the end of the eighteenth century little resembled those of a merchant or artisan 200 years before. As a result of economic development and the dramatic rise of Europe's power that knit the globe more together into a world economy, western Europe sidestepped the threat of a demographic disaster as forecast by Thomas Malthus.

SMITHIAN GROWTH

The impressive growth of the European economy in the seventeenth and eighteenth centuries had little to do with innovations in science or technology or changes in organization or the other fundamental aspects of an industrial revolution outlined in the first chapter. Demand for manufactured goods rose thanks to the "revolutions," but it was satisfied largely through incremental improvements in existing techniques and the intensification of human endeavor, not more revolutionary innovations. Because it is this economy that Adam Smith described so thoroughly, this form of growth is termed "Smithian." Decades of Smithian growth were a necessary but not sufficient precondition for an industrial revolution to occur in late eighteenth century Europe. As late as the publication of *An Inquiry into the Nature and Causes of the Wealth of Nations* in 1776, the possibility that the transformations described in this chapter would culminate in an industrial revolution was still unimagined, much less inevitable.

3

MAKING AN INDUSTRIAL REVOLUTION I: TECHNOLOGICAL CHANGE

If global consumer demand for new, more, and better-quality products was the necessary precondition for an industrial revolution, fulfilling these demands required three major developments. First, newer and more effective technologies were needed to save labor and to permit different products to be made. Second, innovative methods of organizing production and business were essential to improving the quality and quantity of products available. And third, the state had to take an ever-more active role in fostering economic development. Taken together, these three developments transformed industrial practice and furthered the trends of growing European dominance within a world economic system that were already apparent in the seventeenth and eighteenth centuries.

These shifts reflected a unique moment in the world's economic development. The cotton textile sector was able to take advantage of all the earlier revolutions to achieve a level of growth that eventually transformed the entire economy. Textiles pulled the iron and coal sectors in its wake to reach new heights. The breakthrough to an industrial revolution from Smithian growth took place in Great Britain in the late eighteenth century, but other countries were not far behind. This chapter will explore the unique eighteenth-century technological and organizational components of industrialization and what policymakers and entrepreneurs did to foster them.

THE COTTON INDUSTRY

KING COTTON

The industrial revolution first occurred in one key sector: cotton textiles. New machines and new processes were developed to cope with specific problems that had previously slowed down production. In Europe, cotton textiles were an import substitution industry and as such were independent of guild controls; this independence was vital to the ability of this sector to innovate. Until the eighteenth century, cotton goods were available from India and were generally brought in by monopolistic chartered companies (see Chapter 2). It was to displace Indian cottons from European, American, and African markets that western Europeans undertook groundbreaking improvements in their own industrial methods.

Early European attempts to surpass or even successfully imitate Indian cotton goods were unsuccessful. Many European governments tried to support domestic-made goods by banning the import of such goods from India, Persia, and China. In Great Britain, an initial ban passed in 1700 was extended and made more wide-ranging in 1719 thanks to pressure from woolen manufacturers who feared both the competition from and the ever-growing demand for cotton textiles. An English woolens weaver commented that, "no sooner were the East Indian chintz and printed calicoes prohibited from abroad, but some of Britain's unnatural children set all their arts to work, to evade the law of prohibition, to employ people to mimick the more ingenious Indian, and to legitimate the grievance by making it a manufacture."[1]

Cotton could play such an important role because of its unique qualities. Thread spun from cotton is both stronger and easier to use than wool, linen, or silk. These properties make it suitable to machine-based production. Both bleaching and dyeing last longer and are more effective on cotton than on other natural fibers. Cotton fabric is also lighter and more washable than these other mainstay textile fabrics. The potential market for cotton, both in Europe and overseas, was therefore greater than for any other textile.

To produce a bolt of cotton fabric, the raw cotton had to be combed to remove seeds, dirt, and other impurities. Then the raw cotton had to be spun into thread on a spinning wheel, twisted into yarn, and then woven into cloth on a loom. To this basic process, other steps could be added to improve the quality or attractiveness of the cloth. Roving twisted the threads to increase their strength. Cloth could be cleaned and the weave shrunken and thickened by dunking it in a mix of hot water and fuller's earth (or some other cleanser) and then beating it with wooden mallets in a process called fulling. Dyeing or bleaching could help sell the cloth by making it more fashionable or attractive. Treating the fabric in other ways softened it. The production process could be sped up by inventing new machines to save labor or by adding an additional source of power to run more than one machine at a time.

INVENTIONS

Thanks to John Kay, at the dawn of the industrial revolution weaving was more technologically advanced than the other parts of the production process.

In 1733, Kay invented the flying shuttle which eliminated the limitation of an "arm's length" to the width of a cloth. The loom's shuttle was fitted with small wheels set in a wooden groove to allow it to move without inferring with the alternating rise and fall of the warp. This simple device both removed a limiting factor and speeded up weaving considerably.

TINKERING

As a domestic industry in cotton goods emerged in Lancashire, entrepreneurs and workers identified a series of mechanical bottlenecks as they tried to help spinning catch up. To find a workable solution, they tinkered with various machines. Over the course of decades, practical men found practical solutions to the bottlenecks. These solutions transformed the industry and began the industrial revolution. The same process was going on in several regions of Europe, but the English developed more efficient solutions than their competitors.

THE INVENTIONS

The key steps toward mechanizing the manufacture of textiles were taken in the late 1760s. In 1765, James Hargreaves invented the spinning jenny (see insert) and in 1767, Richard Arkwright developed the water frame. Both began to be used in 1768. Arkwright's patent dates from the following year, Hargreaves' from the year after. Hargreaves' invention saved considerable labor, but did not fundamentally alter the production process. Arkwright's machine did. The water frame or throstle was a wooden machine about 32 inches high. A wheel was connected to four pairs of rollers to stretch the roved cotton which was then twisted and wound on spindles placed vertically on the machine.

Arkwright intended the device to be powered by horses, but water power was swiftly found to be far more economical, giving the machine its name. The coarse yarn produced by a water frame was strong and tightly twisted; it was suitable for hosiery and the warp for cotton goods. As we shall soon see, Arkwright implemented his invention with pathbreaking success, but technologically, his machine was little different than several others that had been developed over the previous 30 years. With his spinning or jenny mule (1779), Samuel Crompton, also from Lancashire, vastly increased the utility of both Arkwright's and Hargreave's machines. As the name suggests, this is a hybrid machine. It links the rollers of the water frame to the movable carriage of the jenny to stretch, twist, and wind the thread to create a much stronger and finer product. Not long after its invention, a spinning mule could do 200–300 times the work of a spinning wheel.

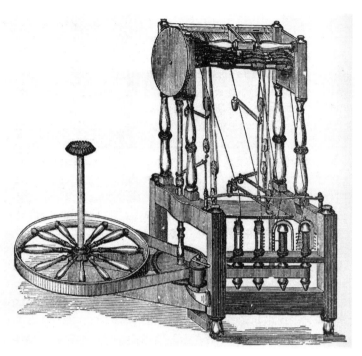

By profession, Arkwright was a barber and a wigmaker. He had no experience in textile manufacture. He learned what he needed to know in his barbershop! This relatively simple machine, built with the help of a clockmaker, was the basis of the transformation of the cotton industry. Arkwright's patent to this machine was revoked in 1785. The British government ruled that he had stolen the idea that made his fortune. The Burndy Library, Cambridge, Massachusetts

This calico printing machine was invented around 1780 and was improved repeatedly for the next 50 years. This version dates from around 1800 and demonstrates the rapidly growing complexity of industrial machinery. The Burndy Library, Cambridge, Massachusetts

James Hargreaves (1720–1778)

Hargreaves was born in Lancashire and spent his first 20 years working as a carpenter and a weaver near Blackburn. As a result, he had both mechanical skills and an intimate knowledge of the process of weaving, although he had little formal education. He was asked by a neighbor, a calico printer named Robert Peel who founded a manufacturing dynasty, to build a carding machine. Not long afterward, legend has it that he saw an overturned spinning wheel that continued to revolve: this image gave him the idea for his jenny. His relatively simple machine consisted of a rectangular frame mounted on four legs with a row of vertical spindles at one end. Two parallel wooden rails were mounted on a carriage that slid back and forth. Cotton that had been carded and roved could then be passed between the two rails and wound on the spindles. A spinner could move the carriage with one hand and turn the handle for the spindles with the other thereby drawing the thread and simultaneously twisting it. The spinning jenny enabled a single worker to replace numerous spinners. Hargreaves' first model had eight spindles, but this number was rapidly increased. A decade later, a spinning jenny could accommodate up to eighty spindles.

Although he successfully solved a vexing technical problem, Hargreaves suffered numerous setbacks in his efforts to profit from his invention. These difficulties were typical of those faced by innovators in this era. Hargreaves only began to construct machines for sale in 1767 and he did not seek a patent for three more years, a decision that would cost him financially. Once it became clear that the spinning jenny saved considerable labor, local cotton spinners who feared for their jobs during a sharp economic downturn, broke down his door, and smashed his machines. Two years later, the same thing happened again. Hargreaves did not seem to fear further violence from rebellious workers, however, because, as the economy improved, he moved out of the frying pan and into the fire. He relocated to Nottingham, a major locus of machine-breaking throughout the eighteenth and nineteenth centuries. Instead Hargreaves experienced far greater difficulties with unscrupulous entrepreneurs and unsympathetic judges. With a partner, he set up a spinning mill that ran successfully for awhile, but his great hope of wealth stemmed from selling his machines. They were cheap to make; they required only a skilled craftsman to make precision parts that moved seamlessly. His problem was that other manufacturers copied it with ease and then refused to pay the patent fees. He sued, but the court found that since his machines had been used before he had patented them, his patent was meaningless. Hargreaves did not die penniless, as another legend has it, he left an estate worth £4,000, but this is a pittance compared to the economic value of his invention. A decade after his death, at least 20,000 spinning jennies were at work in Great Britain with thousands more to be found on the continent of Europe. The device was also swiftly adapted to wool and later linen and silk. Each machine did the work of at least eight people. The spinning jenny completely altered the production of cotton textiles and played a major role in sparking the industrial revolution.

Source: Mantoux, *The Industrial Revolution in the Eighteenth Century*, 216–19, Horn, *The Path Not Taken*, 94, 114, and Berg, *The Age of Manufactures 1700–1820*, 237–39.

Economic Effects

Crompton's jenny mule permitted an enormous increase in the quality and quantity of cotton goods produced. For the first time, a European producer could match the quality and undercut the cost of Indian cotton textiles. A measure of how efficient a labor-saving device the jenny mule was can be seen in a comparison of the hours needed to process 100 pounds of cotton. At the end of the eighteenth century, it took Indian hand spinners more than 50,000 hours, but with Crompton's machine, it took only 2,000 hours. Mechanics, tinkerers, and workers who actually used the machines continuously made further small refinements that, taken together, rapidly improved the initial machines dramatically, thereby increasing their productivity.

Ending a Bottleneck

Additional breakthrough machines followed including the power loom developed by Reverend Edmund Cartwright in 1786. Although a power loom was no faster than a hand-weaver for several decades, a single worker could run first two and then several looms, which sped up production considerably. Frenchman Joseph-Marie Jacquard invented a draw loom capable of imprinting designs and figures on the fabric through the use of punch cards. Developed for use with silk in 1801, the Jacquard loom was applied to all fabrics in the second quarter of the nineteenth century. Richard Roberts applied power to reversing and turning the spindles at varying speeds to create a mule that did not have to be "run" by a human being. He patented the "self-acting" mule in 1825 and improved it greatly 5 years later. Thanks to these innovative machines, what had taken 2,000 hours in the late eighteenth century, dwindled to only 135 hours in 1825.[2] This first bottleneck—spinning—to expanding production was swept aside: these machines saved such prodigious quantities of labor that prices could fall, profits could rise, and demand could be satisfied simultaneously.

Innovations

Other technological developments that eliminated other "bottlenecks" in production facilitated the skyrocketing growth of the cotton industry. American mechanic Eli Whitney developed the cotton gin in 1793 to remove the seeds and dirt from raw cotton. In the 1780s, Arkwright greatly upgraded earlier carding machines that combed and straightened the raw cotton. Finished yarn could be bleached a brilliant white with chlorine using a process developed by French chemist Claude Berthollet in 1784. However, in what would become a frequent occurrence, in 1799, an Englishman made this continental European's discovery more practical and profitable by creating bleaching powder (see Chapter 5). These advances permitted the cotton industry to grow rapidly. Although wool remained the largest European textile industry throughout the eighteenth century, the cotton industry expanded much more quickly. British cotton production increased approximately ten-fold between 1760 and 1800 before spurting in the nineteenth century. By 1830, textiles made of cotton constituted half of all British exports.

IRON, STEEL, AND COAL

IRON AND COAL

Although cotton textiles were the "engine" of economic development, the power of this sector to transform an economy was linked to its influence on other industries. The products of the British iron industry were much in de-mand because of rapid mechanization, improvements in transportation, and the island nation's wartime successes, which helped the prestige of exports. Britain had large deposits of iron ore, but when greater strength or higher quality was needed, they imported ore from countries on the Baltic Sea, par-ticularly Sweden and Russia. Wrought (malleable) iron was generally smelted by combining pig iron (crude cast into ingots known as "pigs") with charcoal, a vegetable fuel that did not transmit impurities to the finished product. In eighteenth-century England, however, charcoal was in short supply because of a general shortage of wood. As a result, roughly one-third of British iron production relocated to the thirteen North American colonies, especially to Pennsylvania, where wood was plentiful as well as easy and cheap to move on the many rivers of the region. The definitive loss of these colonies in 1783 provided a significant cost incentive to the British to further their use of coal as a replacement fuel.

EXPERIMENTATION IN IRON

As in textiles, experimentation by those involved in the production process was the key to improving technique. Iron-masters discovered how to apply heat indirectly. A reverberatory furnace stirred molten pig over a bed of coal until it became wrought iron, but avoided direct contact between the coal and the iron. This process, known as "puddling," was developed by Englishman Henry Cort (1740–1800) in 1783–1784 and perfected in the 1790s. Further improvements made iron produced with coal as fuel of equal or higher quality to traditional production with charcoal while maintaining puddling's huge cost advantage. Cort's methods also permitted 15 tons of iron to be processed in 12 hours. A traditional forge-hammer would be hard pressed to produce a single ton in the same time. These innovations enabled a rapid expansion of iron production in the late 1790s, and even faster growth in the first decades of the nineteenth century as machines made from metal became ever more crucial to economic development. From 23,000 tons produced annually around 1720, by the end of the 1850s, Britain's annual output reached 3.5 million tons.[3]

STEEL

Iron rather than steel was the building block of the industrial revolution. Steel is an iron alloy that contains 1–2% carbon: it is stronger than low-carbon (less than 1%) wrought iron and more malleable than high-carbon (cast or) pig iron. Europeans (among others) had known how to make steel for centuries, but the process of making it was too expensive for widespread use until the 1860s. The major improvement that took place during the eighteenth century was the development of the technique to make crucible or cast steel by Englishman instrument-maker Benjamin Huntsman around 1742. His breakthrough was to mix bars of steel with an alkali in a clay crucible and then heat them with coke. Cast steel had many uses, but it was still expensive and brittle. Only precision instruments, certain tools like files, and some bladed weapons were worth the expense. Although most of the machines that "made" the industrial revolution would have benefited from higher-quality steel construction, iron or wooden construction were much more economical and easier to make. Many of the manufacturing processes of early industrialization were not optimal, but they worked well enough to begin this revolutionary transformation.

COAL

If iron was the material basis of the machines that pumped the lifeblood of the industrial revolution, coal provided the power. Although water, wind, and animals all contributed mightily to the energy used in industrialization, without question, coal took pride of place, especially in Great Britain. Coal had long been of great importance on the British Isles because wood had been a relatively scarce resource since the sixteenth century. British miners were expert at sinking mine shafts, extracting ore, and transporting it. More importantly, British artisans, mechanics, tinkerers, and scientists were accustomed to using coal as a fuel source. A great deal of innovation resulted from the search for ways to use coal as fuel. In 1738, a French inspector of manufacturing toured the coal-mining districts. He was astonished by the variety of different tasks in which coal was used as fuel. "Coal is one of the great sources of richness and abundance in England, and I regard it as the soul of the English manufactures," he reported.[4]

BRITISH ADVANTAGE

This early dependence on coal gave the British essential craft knowledge of coal's properties and the best practices when working with coal. Such knowledge was a major national advantage when technological change and increasingly scarce charcoal forced Britain's competitors on the continent and in North America to switch over to coal. A lack of familiarity with using coal as fuel also made it harder to transfer British technology to other nations.

Even before the age of industrialization, in 1700, British coal production was already at a high level—3 million tons produced annually. From there it skyrocketed, reaching almost 9 million tons by 1775, 22 millions tons in 1815 and, by the end of the 1850s, Britain's output reached nearly 67 million tons annually which represented a staggering two-thirds of global output.[5]

INTERCHANGEABLE PARTS

INTERCHANGEABLE PARTS

Another major source of innovation was the search for interchangeable parts. In an age of handcrafted machines and tools, the notion of manufacturing even the most basic of products with pieces that could be taken from one model and inserted into another was almost impossible to imagine. To apply this goal to something which required precision or moving parts was even more of a pipe dream. Despite the difficulties and expense, military needs led various governments to invest heavily in the project beginning with Bourbon France in the 1750s. Pushed by France's first inspector general of artillery, Jean-Baptiste de Gribeauval, the standardization of components began with large artillery pieces and was applied experimentally to muskets in the late 1770s. The experiment was a technical success, but the gunsmiths' intense opposition to the idea proved a major stumbling block. The idea did not die: Honoré Blanc, an experienced mechanic and gunsmith, was set up in a workshop. In 1791, an experiment was held in which another gunsmith was told to assemble at random a number of gunlocks (the critical piece) from a bin holding enough to make 500 (see insert). It worked, but because of the French Revolution, the experiment was not a prelude to full-scale production. The ideal of interchangeable parts and Blanc's methods were, however, swiftly revived in 1793 soon after the onset of the revolutionary wars. Each part of the process was broken down into as many simple tasks as possible, but again, resistance from the artisans who actually made the guns scuttled the project. At a very leisurely pace considering the depth of the war crisis, Blanc established a large workshop at Roanne in 1794, but only began production 3 years later. In the early years of the nineteenth century, thanks to a hefty government subsidy, Blanc's workshop (he had sold it to another entrepreneur in 1801) produced approximately 10,000 fully interchangeable gunlocks a year—about 5% of the needs of Napoleonic France—at prices only 20% higher than those made by traditional methods.[6] However grudgingly, the era of interchangeable parts had arrived.

ELI WHITNEY

The same needs and the same general process occurred in other nations. Although the British military never attempted interchangeable parts, at least in this period, on the other side of the Atlantic, politicians and entrepreneurs

Honoré Blanc (1736–1801)

Apprenticed to a gunsmith at the age of 12, Blanc rose to become a master armorer in charge of one of France's main arsenals—Saint-Étienne. He designed the main infantry weapon for the French army and was told to standardize tools in all of France's armories. His continued experiments were successful and the government invested millions of *livres* in his efforts to create a means of manufacturing weapons with interchangeable parts. Although Blanc managed to make thousands of gunlocks with interchangeable parts and to train hundreds of skilled workers, his methods had their greatest success under his successor as director in the workshop at Roanne that he formed in 1797. Despite his technical accomplishments, Blanc, the entrepreneur, never made the process economical. When state subsidies stopped, so did the manufacture of gunlocks with interchangeable parts. In this excerpt, he discusses his own efforts in the third person:

> There is no doubt that nothing is of more interest to the state in the manufacture of weapons of war than the greatest economy and the most exact precision . . . [Blanc] has been primarily concerned with the manufacture of gunlocks. He has invented several machines and a great number of dedicated tools for that purpose. The items that make up a gunlock are made separately, but they can be mixed and matched without any danger . . . [The gunlock] will be given definitive shape by machines or standardized measures that cannot vary and that cannot be achieved by a worker's hands. This will create the incalculable advantage permitting the replacement of each part when needed. Thanks to these changes, it will only be necessary to have someone to clean the weapons. Provided that they are well-instructed, one can find someone who can do this anywhere. Blanc will also add that he is personally convinced that the expense of each gunlock will much less than that of those made in the [existing] arms workshops. The expense of reports will also be reduced by half.
>
> The most heinous vice of French arms workshops is that they are run by men who are less interested in service to the nation than in the ways in which they can increase their fortunes.

Source: Honoré Blanc, *Mémoire important sur la fabrication des armes de guerre* (1790). Translated by Jeff Horn.

alike were inspired by the same technological ideals that motivated Gribeauval and Blanc. Eli Whitney, inventor of the cotton gin, seized on a government contract signed in June 1798 to keep his Connecticut-based business afloat. He committed to deliver by the end of September 1800, 10,000 muskets whose parts would be so alike that they could be interchanged. The fact that he had no experience making weapons did not seem to have damaged his confidence. Whitney failed both in achieving interchangeability and in the speed of delivery. The federal government did not receive the guns until January 1809. Although generations of American school children were taught that Whitney invented interchangeable parts, what his experience actually demonstrates is that the U.S. government was willing to invest in technological advances. His experience also highlights the vital role of defense spending in supporting key infant industries. In the first few decades of the nineteenth century, other gunsmiths achieved Whitney's goal and the principle of uniformity with interchangeability as a target was implemented in the manufacture of clocks, locks, furniture, and hardware.[7]

Technological change was essential to the ability of Europeans, led by the British, to satisfy worldwide consumer demand. Without labor-saving devices and ways of harnessing other sources of power, traditional means of production had only limited ability to transform the economy or to take full advantage of the opportunities offered to Europeans in that unique moment in world history. Machines and different power sources permitted improvements to the quality and quantity of manufactured goods offered for sale in the global marketplace. These innovations were complemented by changes in the organization of production and business structures. The state also took an increasing hand in supporting economic development.

This chapter has explored the supply side of the transformation of production. It must not be forgotten, however, that these technological changes had a distinct purpose—they did not take place in a vacuum. Technological change was also insufficient to initiate an industrial revolution by itself; it required other changes to turn the means of producing something into a reality that customers might actually purchase. Building a better mousetrap is not very important unless there is appealing bait or if the mouse cannot see the cheese. These complementary changes will be treated in a separate chapter for ease of reading, but the subject matter is intimately linked to the course of technological change explored here.

4

MAKING AN INDUSTRIAL
REVOLUTION II: THE ELABORATION
OF THE FACTORY SYSTEM

Factories predated the industrial revolution in the sense that large buildings that housed many workers collaborating in the manufacture of some product had existed for centuries. Silks, tapestries, porcelains, weapons, and even some ships were made at sites that qualified as factories. But in the eighteenth century, in order to satisfy the burgeoning market for cotton textiles, a hierarchical management emerged that was interested in implementing mechanization, substituting water or coal for human energy, and a greater division of labor. Such means of maximizing production necessitated a much more thorough control over labor and the work process. These characteristics were the difference between a factory derived from the term "manufacture" and a factory *system*. This shift transformed the means of production.

Reliance on machines led producers to relocate to take advantage of cheap coal or sites where a water wheel could be run. Thus, industrialization was regional rather than national as factories clustered around rivers and coal deposits. These power supplies facilitated a new sort of production that lowered costs. Because of competition both from India and from other European countries, such saving went into reducing prices rather than increasing profits. As a result, cotton goods could be afforded by more people, thereby ultimately increasing potential demand. Lower profit per unit was acceptable when volume was skyrocketing. The creation and spread of the modern factory system within the confines of the British textile sector during the late eighteenth century represented the true beginnings of the industrial revolution.

THE FACTORY SYSTEM

THE FIRST MODERN FACTORY

The first modern factory was a cotton mill at Cromford in Derbyshire created by the inventor Richard Arkwright (1732–1792). When it opened in

1771, it had space for a complete set of machines and was purpose-built to be lit by candle for night work. The machines were run by large water wheels. In 1769, Arkwright had founded a horse-powered workshop not far from Hargreaves' jenny mill in Nottingham to utilize his inventions in partnership with a bar-owner and a banker, but there simply was not enough capital to outfit the manufactory the way he wanted. So, in 1771, he formed an association with two rich hosiers: Jedediah Strutt and Samuel Need helped him to create Cromford. At first, Strutt and Need purchased the entire output of the mill for their stocking and knitting businesses, but, in 1773, the three partners established a weaving workshop to make England's first all-cotton calicoes in imitation of goods imported from India. The technical and financial achievements of these enterprises enabled Arkwright, Strutt, and Need to successfully lobby the government in 1774 to eliminate the tariff on imports of raw cotton established to protect the woolen industry. Arkwright's most persuasive argument was that, "The said manufacture, if not crushed by so heavy a duty, will rapidly increase and find new and effectual employment for many thousand British poor, and increase the revenue of the kingdom."[1]

THE SPREAD OF FACTORIES

Cromford became the model for a huge number of other establishments. It swiftly grew to house several thousand spindles and 300 workers. Only 15 years later, there were 140 Arkwright-type water-powered mills spinning cotton. By 1800, England was home to 900 cotton spinning factories of which 300 were large mills patterned on Arkwright's. A large mill was defined as one that employed more than fifty workers. Almost all of these establishments utilized water power. Initially, few, even unskilled workers sought employment at Cromford because the rural site was picked for maximizing water power not for convenience or ease of access. (Unskilled workers were preferred because they did not have to unlearn other techniques, they did not mind the closer supervision demanded by factory labor, and they were willing to be trained to work the machines.) Arkwright solved the labor problem by accepting a huge number of youthful apprentices from Poor Houses all over Britain. The child and teenage apprentices lived at the mill and were bound to work for Arkwright either until they were eighteen or for seven years, whichever was *longer*!

LANCASHIRE

Arkwright's long-term answer to his labor problem was to return to the region of his birth. He set up his factories in the relatively poor region of Lancashire where domestic industry was well-established. Lancashire also had a large number of small streams and shallow rivers that were perfect for turning water wheels. The region enjoyed excellent access to the sea through the port of Liverpool. By taking on limited partners in various ventures, all

---

Josiah Wedgwood on Anti-Machine Riots in Lancashire (1779)

As one of the great entrepreneurs of the age, Josiah Wedgwood recognized that innovation was not always popular with those who might suffer as a result (for Wedgwood's biography, see chapter 5):

[After running into a group of machine-breakers in the morning] On the same day in the afternoon a capital engine or mill in the manner of Arcrites [Arkwright] and in which he is a partner, near Chorley, was attacked, but from its peculiar position, they could approach to it by one passage only, and this circumstance enabled the owner, with the assistance of a few neighbours, to repulse the enemy and preserve the mill for that time. Two of the mob were shot dead upon the spot, one drowned and several wounded. Accordingly they spent all Sunday and Monday morning in collecting firearms and ammunition and melting their pewter dishes into bullets. They were now joined by the Duke of Bridgewater's colliers and others, to the number, we are told, of eight thousand, and marched by beat of drum and with colours flying to the mill where they had met with a repulse on Saturday. They found Sir Richard Clayton guarding the place with fifty armed invalids [wounded veterans] but this handful were by no means a match for enraged thousands, so they content themselves (the invalids) with looking on, while the mob completely destroyed a set of mills valued at £10,000. This was Monday's employment. On Tuesday morning we heard their drums at about two miles' distance from Bolton, a little before we left the place, and their professed design was to take Bolton, Manchester and Stockport on their way to Cromford, and to destroy all the engines not only in these places, but throughout all England.

Source: Josiah Wedgwood, Letter to Thomas Bentley, October 9, 1779, reproduced in Mantoux, *The Industrial Revolution in the Eighteenth Century*, 402.

---

of which he kept financially separate, Arkwright was able to establish several mills making use of the water frame. He was the first European cotton baron. The mills got larger and larger. The factory at Chorley was the biggest in England with 500 workers. In Manchester, Arkwright engaged 600 workers and built a multistory mill with weavers established on the premises instead of in a separate building.

MACHINE-BREAKING

Not all were pleased by Arkwright's astonishing successes. In 1779, workers in Lancashire sacked and burned the factory at Chorley as part of a generalized attack on machines in cotton mills by disgruntled workers who were concerned that their jobs were threatened by the vast increase in the number of machines used in manufacturing (see insert).

Arkwright was so worried about the threat to his main factory at Cromford that he provided his workers with 1,500 weapons and acquired a battery of cannon to defend the approaches. For additional defenders, he reached out to the local men of the neighborhood whose livelihood or that of their families depended on the mill. He proclaimed that, "Five or six thousand men, miners, etc. can at any time be assembled in less than an hour."[2] He need not have worried; British army regulars stationed in Liverpool easily dispersed the rioters.

PATENT PROBLEMS

If the British government came to Arkwright's rescue in 1779, that would not be the case 2 years later when he sued nine other manufacturers for patent infringement. These entrepreneurs successfully challenged Arkwright's claim to have "invented" the water frame, which led the government to suspend the patent. Arkwright again tried to protect his patent in 1783, but first, he took the precaution of mobilizing a number of big name supporters including James Watt (see insert) to champion his claims. This time he was successful, but 2 years later a group of spinners combined to dispute Arkwright's patent by bringing forth the true inventor, a workman named Thomas Highs, who had known Arkwright 15 years before. His machine had been constructed by the same clockmaker who constructed Arkwright's patented water frame. The jury swiftly returned a verdict that condemned Arkwright and supported the actions of his competitors.

ARKWRIGHT AS ENTREPRENEUR

Nothing succeeds like success. Despite having been convicted of patenting someone else's design, Arkwright became the richest cotton spinner in Great Britain and swiftly rose to political and social prominence. He created a number of important factories including New Lanark (see Chapter 2) and he is credited with being the first to use steam power to run a factory in 1786 (see below). Arkwright was knighted the same year and he soon became the Sheriff of the County of Derby. Not only was this an important post for overseeing public order in this burgeoning industrial district, but it marked the acceptance of Arkwright by the local elite: he was one of them. When he died in 1792, he left a fortune valued at more than £500,000. This greedy, dishonest man was one of the great entrepreneurs and managers of the era; he put together the ideas of a number of others to create a new manufacturing process, thereby beginning the modern factory age.

STEAM ENGINE

The development of the steam engine is an important part of the story of the industrial revolution. It harnessed Britain's iron and coal resources and enabled entrepreneurs to substitute capital for labor on a systematic basis. The steam engine was developed in the late seventeenth century. In 1712, Thomas Newcomen created the piston-driven coal-powered steam

James Watt (1736–1819)

Born in Greenlock, Scotland, Watt was largely self-educated. At the age of 19, he went to London to become a mathematical instrument-maker. In 1757, he was appointed the instrument-maker for the University of Glasgow. Watt became interested in steam engines because he had to repair the university's model of a Newcomen engine. During the 1760s, Watt was supported financially by English inventor John Roebuck. He used that time to experiment with improving the efficiency of existing steam engines. His first patent, issued in 1769, had a separate condensing chamber that both improved steam pressure on the piston and removed the need to cool the cylinder, thereby preventing heat loss and maximizing fuel use.

A new phase in Watt's career began in 1775 when Matthew Boulton (1728–1809) purchased Roebuck's interest in Watt's engine. Boulton and Watt began to manufacture engines at the Soho Engineering Works in Birmingham. Over the next several years, Watt developed several other innovations including introducing pistons that moved up and down (a reciprocal motion), which could drive machines such as the power loom through the addition of a rod and crank, which turned in a circle (rotary motion). In addition, Watt implemented a double-acting system in which steam was admitted alternately to both ends of the cylinder to drive pistons. Finally, Watt developed a "steam governor" which automatically regulated the speed of an engine by linking output to input, a concept that is fundamental to automation. Boulton and Watt's first engine, installed in 1776, pumped water from a coal mine.

Boulton and Watt guarded their monopoly fiercely. Both Boulton and Watt came to conceive of themselves as scientists, joining and participating faithfully in several different learned societies. This activity enhanced their national and international reputations and assisted in the sale of their engines while also ensuring their value to the state which protected their patent rights.

In 1800, Boulton and Watt's patent rights expired and Watt retired from business. At this point, Britain had more than 500 operational Boulton and Watt steam engines. Several dozen more had been sold on the continent and a significant number of copies of their design had been made in places where English patent rights could not be enforced. Watt's designs and willingness to oversee the quality of the machines greatly enhanced the efficiency of the steam engine, paving the way for further improvements and facilitating the mechanization so fundamental to the Industrial Revolution. As a sign of his importance to the study of efficiency and power, an electrical unit of measurement, the watt, was named after him. This designation also recognized that it had been Watt who coined the term "horsepower" to describe the energy output of an engine.

pump which became a practical, albeit expensive, tool for draining coal mines and swamps and delivering water to fountains in large cities like London and Paris. Because Newcomen's engine only converted about 1% of the thermal energy in steam into mechanical energy, it could only be used in places with access to plentiful, cheap coal.

As coal mines tapped deeper veins of coal, they were dependent on steam engines to draw out the water that was a constant threat to the integrity of the tunnels. Since steam engines ran on coal, the relationship was symbiotic. But the need for so many engines burning so much coal had a devastating environmental impact on coal-mining districts. The Burndy Library, Cambridge, Massachusetts

Improving the steam engine occupied many of Britain's best engineers. The most successful ones were experienced in designing and building precision tools. In the 1760s, John Smeaton (1724–1792), an instrument-maker from Leeds, upgraded existing designs, doubling their efficiency. James Watt (1736–1819), an instrument-maker in Glasgow, spent two decades tinkering with the engine, solving several technical problems. His first patent was in 1769 and the final version of his engine was unveiled in 1778. Watt's engine saved a huge amount of coal and permitted the machine to be moved. Although he is often credited with inventing the steam engine, his actual achievement was to make them applicable to many more tasks and to point the way toward further improvements. A contemporary scientist explained the new calculations an entrepreneur faced in deciding how to invest in a power source:

The daily work of a horse is equal to that of five or six men . . . The expense of keeping a horse is generally twice or thrice as great as the hire of a day labourer, so that the force of horses may be reckoned about half as expensive as that of men . . . On the authority of Mr. Boulton a bushel (84 lbs) of coal is equivalent to the daily labour of 8 1/3 men or perhaps more; the value of this quantity of coal is seldom more than that of the work of a single labourer for a day, but the expense of machinery renders a steam-engine somewhat more than half as expensive as the number of horses for which it is substituted.[3]

An Improved Steam Engine

British entrepreneurs and craftsmen rapidly applied this engine to run all sorts of industrial machines. The utility of Boulton and Watt engines was limited by their large size and their lack of sufficient pressure to perform certain tasks. Liberated by the expiration of Watt's patent, another Englishman, Richard Trevithick, developed a more efficient means of using the available energy in 1800. He then went on to build the first high-pressure engines. This innovation made it possible to build steamboats and railroads, the era's most vital advances in transportation, as well as more powerful tools for industry.

Steam and Factories

The development of the modern factory is often linked to the steam engine. As the previous discussion demonstrates, steam power was not essential to the first factories. It was not until 1783 that steam power was first used in factory, albeit indirectly. Arkwright's Manchester mill used a Newcomen engine to pump water to drive the machines in the dry season when the water pressure was insufficient to turn the waterwheel. The first truly steam-driven factory was at Papplewick, Nottinghamshire and began operation in 1785. Watt wrote to his partner, Matthew Boulton, "If you come home by way of Manchester, please do not seek orders for cotton-mill engines, because I hear that there are so many mills erecting on powerful streams in the North of England, that the trade must soon be overdone, and consequently our labour may be lost."[4] Other sources of power did not disappear or even fade away as the efficiency of steam engines improved.

For decades, steam did not represent a huge improvement over other sources of power. All but a few of the 496 Boulton and Watt engines sold by that firm produced only 15–16 horsepower per hour. They were limited by the current state of metalwork which could not fabricate parts capable of withstanding greater steam pressure. Thus, for decades, a steam engine did not provide appreciably more power than wind or water could generate. Until the dawn of the nineteenth century, the steam engine's great advantage was its mobility and its independence of the weather.[5] However, the enormous investment in steam engines and the mechanization it permitted did encourage a round-the-clock use of the machines. Constant use of the machines by two shifts of workers had dramatic effects on total output and heightened the need to discipline the labor force to get them to accept nightwork. The true age of steam in manufacturing did not begin until after 1800 when Watt's patent expired. By 1835, three-quarters of the machines in the cotton industry were run by steam.[6]

In addition to its traditional spheres of agriculture and mining, and its new home in textile mills and iron foundries, steam power was applied to run a host of other machines. Matthew Boulton set up six presses to make coins for the Mint. Brewers and canal-masters used steam engines primarily as pumps. Others were interested in transportation. William Murdock, a Boulton and Watt employee devised a steam-driven wheeled carriage (see Chapter 8). In 1801, Henry Bell began to experiment with a steamboat (based on successful French experiments undertaken in 1783), and a decade later, he established a steamer on the Clyde River. Steamships required constant pressure to supply the motive power. These lessons were applied later to the steam locomotive which was the key to the railroad and commenced a revolution in land transport.

LIMITATIONS OF THE "NEW PRODUCTION"

This emphasis on machines, alternative forms of power, and the emergence of the factory system must not obscure how limited a place in the overall economy these new means of production occupied during the industrial revolution. Alfred D. Chandler Jr. has argued influentially that large factories had an inevitable advantage over other forms of production because of the efficiencies of scale and scope that could be engendered. However, this analysis has been found to fit only the peculiar characteristics of the American economy rather than the European roots of modern industrialism (see Chapter 6). Chandler's argument about factories cannot explain why dispersed production remained the norm for most manufactured goods, even in textiles, well into the nineteenth century. For many decades, the putting-out system or the urban sweatshops that produced tailored goods, stationary or seasonal products existed alongside and even complemented factory production. Nor, as we have seen, were the first factories, the gigantic "dark satanic mills" immortalized by the poet William Blake. As late as 1835, the entire United Kingdom boasted only 1,330 woolen mills, 1,245 cotton factories, 345 flax mills, and 238 silk factories. The average number of workers in cotton mills was 167 and only 59 in woolens. The figure for cottons is distorted by the existence of some gigantic firms: only 10% of firms had more than 100 workers. Even in 1871, the average number of employees in British manufacturing was under 20.[7] Economic historians have increasingly focused on different aspects of the production process rather than concentrate solely on factories to help explain the phenomenal economic successes recorded by the industrial revolution.

BUSINESS EFFICIENCIES

A NEW FORM OF GROWTH

At least two major interdependent trends in production came together in the industrial revolution. The first stressed the use of machines gathered together into factories and relied on nonorganic sources of energy. The other trend was an outgrowth of experiences with domestic industry and involved an intensification of both management and labor in the production process. This trend was independent of the rise of the factory system, but contributed mightily to its success. In one sense, this trend can be understood as the modernization of the techniques that generated Smithian growth.

ENTREPRENEURIALISM

Organization remained the watchword of production. Entrepreneurs earned their money by finding market niches to exploit, developing marketing strategies for local, regional, national, and foreign consumption, attracting sufficient investment capital, maintaining adequate reserves, arranging credit, hiring managers and workers, and investing in innovation or upkeep, all while overseeing production and the workforce. They also lobbied the government and interacted with local elites to garner protection from workers, competitors, and foreign challenges.

AN UNCERTAIN ENVIRONMENT FOR MANAGERS

Entrepreneurs faced a thoroughly uncertain business climate. Business schools had not yet emerged. Neither on the job training nor apprenticeship could teach people how to market, manage labor, or perform the kinds of complex accounting that would allow an entrepreneur to analyze costs and prices while planning for depreciation and the need to phase investment. The computational skills and means of accounting simply did not yet exist and would not for more than a century! As a result, bankruptcy was a constant threat. This threat was especially daunting because the legal system imprisoned people for petty debt. As a result, knowledge took a backseat to trustworthiness in the skill set of a successful entrepreneur. A British foundry owner commented on what he looked for in a manager: "character, capacity and technical knowledge ... are the three essentials, and I have placed them in the order of their importance ... In the choice of your subordinates the same general principles would be observed. Character is the first requisite, cleverness and skill in his craft the second."[8] Frequently, the best-trained, most innovative, and most professional managers were the children of the founders of a business who were raised to run the enterprise.

RISK

Ensuring a sufficient stock of capital or adequate credit were even more important thanks to the uncertainties of shipping schedules in an age of sail. The need to wait long periods while goods were shipped around the world and then transported to their outlets also meant that entrepreneurs had to have even more working capital than would seem necessary today. With the insurance sector in its infancy, entrepreneurs had to assess risk with incomplete information, insufficient tools, and no training other than a classical education and perhaps an apprenticeship. Those with the knack and a great deal of luck could make a killing, those who did not ended up in prison, impoverished, or at the least, unsuccessful. Sir Benjamin Truman, a brewer who created a mass market for his brand of beer wrote: "There can be no other way of raising a great Fortune but by carrying on an Extensive Trade. I must tell you young Man, this is not to be obtained without Spirrit and great application. . . ."[9] Being an entrepreneur in the early industrial revolution was not for the lazy or faint of heart.

LIMITING RISK

The available techniques of limiting risk and finding sufficient capital were well known. Entrepreneurs found partners and secured loans. The best partners and lenders had a tie or relationship that bound them. Whether it was a family member, someone who shared an interest or the solidarity of someone of the same religious faith or ethnic group or even just someone who had attended the same school or lived in the neighborhood, finding a reason to trust your partner was essential to forming a lasting business. Until 1852, British law did not permit a limited form of liability that distinguished between active partners who directed the firm and passive partners who provided capital, but were not involved in management: small investments could easily lead to bankruptcy. Of the various links, kinship was by far the most important: the family firm was the prototypical form of business organization. Shared religious faith was a distant second among ties. A mutual short-term desire to make a profit or a similar approach to risk or business practice was useful, but not essential to successful partnerships and lending arrangements. As discussed earlier, joint-stock companies did exist, but they were extremely few in number because they needed to be authorized by the state and such firms generated a minuscule proportion of industrial output.

BORROWING

Borrowing money was just as difficult as finding a stable, useful, long-term partner. A key difference was the existence of a more formal and growing banking sector that helped to keep capital in circulation at reasonable rates of interest. The emergence of a sophisticated mortgage market for land also contributed to the availability of capital for productive purposes. The stability of the mercantilist English government, the profits of the empire, and the continuing growth of trade combined with the institutional development of the nascent banking system to lower interest rates dramatically. In 1700, annual interest rates were about 6%, but this fell to 3.5% a year around mid-century. Between 1714 and 1832, the English government prohibited commercial interest rates above 5% a year. In France, Britain's chief industrial competitor, interest rates never dipped below 5% and even relatively safe investments in turbulent or isolated regions could pay a great deal more than that. Thus, Britons enjoyed the cheapest and most plentiful credit in the world.

CAPITAL/ASSETS RATIO

Access to cheap credit available for long periods was a major British advantage in the race to initiate an industrial revolution. A typical firm had less than one-quarter of its assets in fixed goods like the building, machines and tools. About 20% was in raw materials and stock while the remaining capital—the bulk of the company's assets—was in trade debt: goods that had been shipped, but not yet paid for. These percentages take on even greater weight when the sums involved are considered. Jedediah Strutt established a cotton-spinning factory at Belper in 1793: it cost £5,000 to erect the building, another £5,000 for various machines (including, but not restricted to improved Arkwright water frames) and another £5,000 for stocks of raw materials. A flax spinning mill set up by William Marshall in Leeds that same year cost £14,000 to get off the ground.[10] As machines got bigger and more expensive thanks to technological innovation, the start-up costs and capital requirements increased proportionately.

SELF-MADE MEN?

The stories used to exhort workers to maximum effort of successful artisans rising to become factory owners were more fables than fact. The self-made man was part of the heroic story of the industrial revolution created for propaganda purposes that is still told by far too many people. In 1799, Matthew Boulton told a Select Committee that, "all the manufacturers I have ever known began the world with very little capitals." It is hard to credit this statement. Boulton inherited a large and prosperous silver smithing business from his father and married a woman with a dowry of £28,000![11]

"PLOUGHING BACK" THE PROFITS

Once an enterprise was established, expansion was generally financed by "ploughing back" the partners' profits rather than by raising new capital. This characteristic of business practice earned the description "family capitalism." A consequence of this means of financing was that capital-intensive innovations were generally long delayed and sometimes avoided altogether. The entrepreneurs of the industrial revolution did not uniformly or systematically maximize profit. As we shall see in Chapter 5, this same lack of investment might also be attributed to the British state which allowed transportation facilities and public investment in schools and hospitals to lag severely behind other European countries. These deficiencies were true everywhere but was especially noticeable in the industrial districts.

SUBCONTRACTING

Subcontracting was an important means used by entrepreneurs to limit their need for both capital and labor. Sometimes the subcontractor was an artisan like a gunsmith who made something that took considerable skill or craft knowledge. In other sectors like woolens, it was the most labor-intensive tasks like cloth mending that were outsourced. The heavy reliance on subcontracting also helps to explain how small-scale artisanal enterprise and domestic industry could complement the emerging factory system. All boats rose together. These styles of production were not truly in competition. Small shops also generated useful technological innovations that could be adopted by larger manufactures. The "flexible specialization" of the small producer of luxuries or handmade products could also be a separate source of economic growth that helped to create demand for mass-produced goods. The prevalence of subcontracting also blurs the distinctions that many contemporary economists make between small-scale and large-scale enterprise, particularly with regard to the uses of technology. In practice, it was and is never that simple to determine the best scale of an enterprise to appropriately use technology.

LABOR OVERSIGHT

All the tasks discussed above were vital to successful entrepreneurs, but one area of activity was even more essential to ensuring profitability: overseeing labor. Finding ways to save labor, that is, to lessen the amount of labor needed to produce something was a direct way that management could improve profitability. During the initial decades of the industrial revolution, implementing labor saving was probably the most important function of managers and entrepreneurs. As demonstrated in the previous chapter, technology was a critical element of labor-saving, but as we shall see, it was far from the only one.

MANAGING THE WORKFORCE

DIVISION OF LABOR

Adam Smith was one of the first great proponents of increasing the division of labor. Instead of one person making something from start to finish, the principle of the division of labor was to break down the process of manufacturing into as many simple, easily repeated, separate tasks as possible, and then developing mechanical aids to ensure the speed and reliability of production. Workers would become expert in this task and could focus all their attention on it, lessening the time it took them. Smith's famous example was pin-making which could be broken down into eighteen different operations:

I have seen a small manufactory of this kind where ten men only were employed, and where some of them consequently performed two or three distinct operations. But though they were very poor, and therefore but indifferently accommodated with the necessary machinery, they could, when they exerted themselves, make among them twelve pounds of pins in a day.

Whereas a novice could not make more than 20 pins by themselves in a day, those twelve pounds represented about 48,000 pins made by these trained workers "in consequence of a proper division and combination of their operations."[12] The increase in production and the labor-saving potential of the division of labor were apparent to all entrepreneurs, but concrete and detailed knowledge of the production process was necessary to achieve it. Not all manufacturers had such knowledge, but there were other, more obvious ways to save labor.

SUBSTITUTION OF LABOR

A vital part of the process of industrialization was the substitution of women and children for more expensive (and more truculent) male labor. Women and children were always paid less to perform the same tasks. The use of machines was generally reserved for a small cadre of skilled male laborers because it was claimed that the devices required greater physical strength to use—this assertion was only partly true—while the bulk of other tasks benefited from the more dexterous fingers of women and children. In economic terms, this reversal of the gender division of domestic industry deskilled the labor force and permitted a thoroughgoing substitution of capital for labor.

Women and children were the bulk of the labor force in the cotton textile sector during the first century of industrialization. A British survey undertaken in 1818 found that women comprised a little over half the workers in cotton textiles with children representing another third. In Scotland, the reliance on women and girls was even greater. Female labor, overwhelmingly women under thirty, especially teenagers, made up over 60% of the cotton workers in Glasgow and approached 70% in worksites situated outside urban areas.[13] The labor of women made the cotton textile industry productive and profitable.

CHILDREN

Children labored at least as much as women. In 1851, a commission found that one-third of children under the age of fifteen worked outside the home. This figure drastically underrepresented the number of children in the workforce because it did not count those employed in domestic industry or agriculture.[14] *At least* half of nominally school-age children worked full-time during the industrial revolution.

OPPRESSION OF CHILDREN

Nor was the labor of children entered into voluntarily. Parents could commit their children to work. This was not just the standard use of juveniles to perform domestic chores or to help their parents. Destitute parents sent their children up to the age of 21 out to work for the parish in exchange for support. A parent could also apprentice their child for 7 years to a master or entrepreneur. In neither case could the child leave or do anything about their working conditions. From the age of 4 or 5, children worked the same 12- to 14-hour shifts as adults and they suffered disproportionately from the unhealthy and dangerous working conditions. In a study of 609 examples of enforcing discipline or modifying the behavior of factory children undertaken in 1833, nearly 95% of all the tactics used were negative, with dismissal being the norm (58%), with fines (17%), corporal punishment (9%), and threats (8%) also being common. A reward was given only twenty-three times (4%), a promotion or raise nine times (1%) and kindness twice.[15]

INDENTURE

In his memoirs, the legal reformer Sir Samuel Romilly (1757–1818) observed that the conditions for many children strongly resembled the indentured adult laborers sent out to the colonies to labor for a fixed number of years in exchange for their passage. This practice was common during the seventeenth and early eighteenth centuries:

It is a very common practice with the great populous parishes in London to bind children in large numbers to the proprietors of cotton-mills in Lancashire and Yorkshire, at a distance of 200 miles. The children, who are sent off by wagon loads at a time, are as much lost for ever to their parents as if they were shipped off for the West Indies. The parishes that bind them, by procuring a settlement for the children at the end of forty days, get rid of them for ever; and the poor children have not a human being in the world to whom they can look up for redress against the wrongs they may be exposed to from these wholesale dealers in them, whose object it is to get everything that they can possibly wring from their excessive labour and fatigue.[16]

Parliament did not limit such appointments until 1816, when a 40-mile limit was imposed. Other attempts were made to improve the lives of children, but the first measure to have any real effect was the Factory Act of 1833 (passed, not coincidentally, the same year that Britain prohibited slavery) which outlawed work for children under the age of 9 and limited it for children aged 9–13 to 8 hours per day. Night work was forbidden. The measure also restricted children aged 14–18 to working a mere 12 hours a day. Thus, until the closing decades of the industrial revolution, children could be and were exploited in huge numbers.

The passage of this Act occasioned a storm of protests from mill-owners all over Britain. They complained to the House of Commons that such limitations were "prejudicial to the Cotton Trade" and "impracticable" because "Free labourers cannot be obtained to perform the night work, but upon very disadvantageous terms to the manufacturers." Mill-owners also noted that the law separated the shifts of parents and children, masters and apprentices, and the majority of workers from their assistants which harmed productivity and made the supervision of children more difficult.[17]

WOMEN'S WAGES

The deliberate and systematic substitution of the labor of women and children represented a considerable savings. In the mid-nineteenth century, in the capital of the British cotton industry—the city of Manchester—the highest paid female factory worker made a quarter of what the highest paid male laborer earned. The *lowest* paid male worker made 13–15 shillings a week while the *highest* paid female workers earned 7–11 shillings.[18] It should be mentioned that these wages were perhaps 20% higher than nonfactory wages; they had to be to get skilled or free labor to accept the harsh discipline and unpleasant working conditions of the factories.

CHILDREN'S WAGES

Children earned far less. Apprentices and parish appointees worked mostly for room, board and a mostly hypothetical training in the techniques appropriate to the industry. At best, they made one-sixth to one-eighth the wages of an adult worker and suffered not just "the slings and arrows of outrageous fortune," but the straps, whips, and fists of their overseers. Corporal punishment was considered necessary to make "lazy" children work 12 or 14 hours a day. In 1832, a colonial slave-owner testified before House of Commons that: "I have always thought myself disgraced by being the owner of slaves, but we never in the West Indies thought it possible for any human being to be so cruel as to require a child of nine years to work twelve and a half hours a day, and that, you acknowledge, is your regular practice."[19]

PRODUCTIVITY OF LABOR

A third essential element of management's task was to increase the productivity of labor. Although oversight was not as thorough as in a small workshop, an important task of full-time overseers and managers ensured that laborers did not simply punch the clock, but worked as hard as they could throughout their shift. This was frustrating task. As a whole, entrepreneurs were dissatisfied with their employees' work habits: "The poor [laborer] in the manufacturing counties will never work any more time in general than is necessary just to live and support their weekly debauches," said a wool clothier about the West Country.[20] As much as possible, managers wanted laborers to be able to match the regularity and stamina of the machines they tended. Managers resorted to a variety of disciplinary measures that ranged from docking the pay of workers who did not give their best effort to heavy doses of corporal punishment.

DISCIPLINE

Another aspect of the growing effort to discipline the workforce focused on getting workers to show up on time, every day, and to remain at their stations the entire day. This was not as easy as it sounds when customary practice ran contrary. A hosier named Isaac Cookson remarked in 1806 that: "I find the utmost distaste on the part of the men, to any regular hours or regular habits ... The men themselves were consistently dissatisfied because they could not go in & out as they had been used to do.... "[21] Another problem was that when workers labored six days a week, their day of "rest"— Sunday—was often punctuated by blowing off a little steam, often by drinking to excess. "Saint Monday" was the term used when workers failed to come to work after a binge. Even Tuesday was a slow day for those recovering from a particularly intense drunk. Managers also wanted to cut down drastically the number of holidays, religious or otherwise, both paid and unpaid, to keep the machines humming. When the workday usually took ran from dawn to dusk and clocks and watches were not yet common possessions, it was difficult to ensure punctuality, especially for early morning shifts. In 1823, a spinner in a Lancashire cotton mill located near Manchester faced the following penalties during his 14-hour workday:

	shillings	pence
Any spinner found with his window open	1	0
Any spinner found dirty at his work	1	0
Any spinner found washing himself	1	0
Any spinner leaving his oil can out of place	1	0
Any spinner putting his gas[-light] out too soon	1	0
Any spinner spinning with gaslight too long in the morning	2	0
Any spinner heard whistling	1	0
Any spinner being five minutes late after last bell rings	1	0
Any spinner going further than the roving-room door when fetching rovings	1	0
Any spinner being sick and cannot find another spinner to give satisfaction must pay for steam per day	6	0
Any spinner having a little waste on his spindles	1	0[22]

INDUSTRIOUSNESS

The managerial obsession with time and industry was not just about profit. It should also be understood as the application of the same habits of industriousness learned by the middle classes during the preceding centuries to the working classes. As such, the imposition of these forms of discipline to create a new, more productive industrial laborer was seen as both a mission and a vocation by dedicated social reformers and not just as an essential part of maximizing profit. It is no coincidence that many of the most devoted advocates of temperance and abstinence for the working classes were entrepreneurs and their families.

The factory was at the heart of this disciplinary effort, but it took place in smaller-scale workshops as well.

INDIVIDUALISM IN INDUSTRY

From the perspective of a manager or entrepreneur, discipline also implied an individual relationship between master and man. In other words, the

This reproduction of cloth manufacturer Samuel Wethergill of Philadelphia's engraved copperplate was used as early as 1782. This clean and tidy woman is hard at work amid the virgin lands of the New World demonstrating how virtue and industry were one and the same. The Burndy Library, Cambridge, Massachusetts managers did not want any kind of union, coalition, or association to join workers together to contest or resist their demands. As individuals, unskilled workers had to give in—their strength was only in numbers. So managers attacked these organizations, breaking them whenever and however possible. They also took aim at customary work practices that, to their way of thinking, prevented innovation and slowed down efficiency. Managers resented attempts by groups of workers to influence hiring and firing practices and work floor rules and regulations. During the industrial revolution, managers demanded that their workers function as a blank slate upon which they could impose their own standards, practices, and expectations.

Pioneers like Arkwright found the task of "training human beings to renounce their desultory habits of work, and identify themselves with the unvarying regularity of the complex automaton" a difficult proposition at best.[23] When workers complained, the burgeoning population allowed unskilled laborers to be replaced with impunity. When and where that proved to be difficult, laborers were imported from other, poorer areas such as Ireland or the Highlands of Scotland to fill the jobs that no local person would take. During the first two or three generations trained to the factory, the new industrial discipline was imposed, in many cases on workers who were not free to dispose of their own labor; modern notions of discipline were not accepted passively. The frequent resort to violence—judicial and military—on the part of the state to enforce industrial discipline or to protect innovating entrepreneurs demonstrates how deeply changes in customary work practice were resented by laborers whose militancy threatened the entire economic, social, and political order (see Chapter 5).

WORKERS' RESPONSES

The reaction of workers to industrial discipline varied widely. There were certainly a large number of laborers who accepted their new situations and made the best of it. Workers tried to innovate or get ahead in some way and to use the system to their advantage. Others went along grudgingly, often because they had no other alternative, but they tolerated their situation. A significant number, however, felt they were being taken advantage of and resisted the labor demands of the industrial revolution, at least to some degree. For many, resistance took the form of emigration, often to the United States. For others, the traditional labor tactics of coalition and combination, slowdown and strike were used to resist workplace innovation or to preserve customary practices. In some trades, in some times, and in some places, these tactics had considerable success, at least in the short term. Other laborers turned to more "modern" forms of resistance and complaint such as politics and/or unions. To understand the process of industrialization, particularly the lessons that can be drawn for contemporary business practice, the complaints of the workers must be examined and taken seriously rather than dismissed as "traditional" or "irrational."

EXPLOITATION

Workers justifiably resented many aspects of the process of industrialization. Entrepreneurs and labor forces always have certain areas of conflict, but the emergence of a hierarchical and centralized system of management responsible for the production, distribution, and sale of manufactured goods was especially frustrating from the perspective of workers. The increasing complexity of the economic system, the growing division of labor, and the spread of the tentacles of the new economy around the world all combined to alienate the people who actually made the goods from economic decision making. Nor did laborers retain any true control or even influence over the production process.

Workers looked at or looked back on smaller-scale production as an economic system where masters and men coordinated their efforts and where a worker could take pride in seeing something designed, made, and sold. The growing division of labor also made it more and more difficult for a laborer to understand the entire production process well enough to strike out on their own and become an entrepreneur in their own right. Adam Smith was one of the first to note that the division of labor was a two-edged sword. While it is more productive, it is also more stultifying. As workers' "whole life is spent in performing a few simple operations . . . He naturally loses, therefore becomes as stupid and ignorant as it is possible for a human creature to become." Instead of coming to resemble a machine, "His dexterity at his own particular trade seems, in this manner, to be acquired at the experience of his intellectual, social, and martial virtues."[24] For skilled laborers, industrialization also closed off many of the avenues to social mobility previously open to them. Nor could they leave; until 1824, the emigration of many categories of skilled laborer was legally forbidden by the British government.

UNEMPLOYMENT

The frequent recourse to firing recalcitrant workers and the enormous numbers of jobs made redundant by mechanization also angered the laboring classes. The argument that the total number of industrial jobs was increasing was accurate, but as the shifting sex and age breakdown of the factory workers demonstrates, those who got the new jobs were not the same people who were being laid off. Technological and managerial obsolescence combined to render whole segments of the working classes without a means of earning a living.

The imposition of industrial discipline was also a major bone of contention between masters and men. The elimination of holidays, the increasing length of the workday and work week and following the dictates of the clock were innovations that impinged on the free time, independence, and customary practice of a huge proportion of the population. In some sectors, the institution of payment by output but with regularly increased quotas, rather than payment by the hour was also detested. Workers believed that this form of remuneration destroyed their control over workplace rhythms and ignored the differences in energy and outlook that stem from the passage of the seasons. Nor did workers like the recourse to corporal punishment especially against women and children. The fact that employers also attempted to destroy or prevent any attempt at labor organization to redress grievances also irked workers who believed rightly that their customary rights and traditional protections were being trampled on.

PROFITS RESENTED

The purpose of this discipline—greater profits for entrepreneurs and investors—was perhaps the greatest source of outrage by workers. A group of cotton spinners employed by Charles Lacy of Nottingham protested his innovations in 1811: "It appeareth to us that the said Charles Lacy was actuated by the most diabolical motives, namely to gain riches by the misery of his Fellow Creatures."[25] They felt that if they were contributing to the greater efficiency of production and sacrificing their leisure time, independence, and health, then they should enjoy a proportionate share of the profits. Lacy cheated his customers by selling shoddy goods and worked his employees for long hours at little pay: these anonymous protesters sentenced Lacy to death. An 1818 public address distributed by a group of workers whose wages had been lowered because of an agreement made by a coalition of employers made a similar case, but without the threat of violence: "though we work six days and make long hours, on an average the Mule Spinners cannot earn half a proper subsistence ... while their employers gain immense profits."[26] It was abundantly clear to industrial laborers that entrepreneurs and managers achieved the breakthrough to an industrial society at their expense.

LOWERING WAGES

The habit of laying off employees and lowering the price for labor whenever sales lagged was symptomatic of entrepreneurial attitudes toward industrial workers. In 1799, a national association of cotton weavers centered in Lancashire complained of the misery caused by the reduction of wages. Seven years earlier, a weaver earned 22 shillings for producing 44 yards of cloth. Now, they earned only half that for making 60 yards of a significantly higher-quality fabric. A petition stated: "It is in vain to talk of bad trade [poor sales]; if goods are actually not wanted, they cannot be sold at any price; if wanted, 2d. [2 pence] or 3d. per yard will not stop the buyer; and whether does it appear more reasonable that 2d. or 3d. per yard should be laid on the consumer, or taken from the labourer?"[27]

The revival of customary means of ensuring a living known as a minimum wage below which salaries could not be lowered was widely discussed at this time. At the request of merchants and manufacturers, however, Parliament increasingly abrogated such protections over the course of the eighteenth century. Establishing a legal minimum wage or fixing some relationship between wage levels and the price of food were both rejected out of hand by the government as being too binding on manufacturers and potentially injurious to the national economy: the struggle against revolutionary and then Napoleonic France was used to justify the continuing sacrifices demanded of the working classes. Nothing was said about when or if wages would return to previous levels.

THE WORK ENVIRONMENT

At the same time that industrial wages were being reduced to—or even below—the poverty line, workers were angry that through neglect, the work environment was increasingly unhealthy. Water-logged mine shafts, closed rooms full of wool particles, breathing coal dust, difficult repetitive motions, badly constructed machines, dangerous raw materials (toxic materials like mercury, lead, arsenic, and chlorine were commonly used in many industries), and extremes of heat and cold were all magnified by exhaustion and poor diet. These environmental conditions led directly to pneumonia, arthritis, rheumatism, bursitis, carpal tunnel syndrome, eye strain, and tuberculosis. Machines sheared off fingers and explosions led to the loss of legs. Mine collapses and falls left battered and broken bodies behind them. Chemical poisoning left people paranoid and palsied. The effects of these conditions on pregnant women and children were even more pronounced. In 1831, a medical doctor, Turner Thakrah explored health issues in the factories. Observing the stream of factory workers flowing past him outside Manchester, he commented: "Here I saw, or thought I saw, a degenerate race—human beings stunted, enfeebled, and depraved—men and women that were not be aged—children that were never to be healthy adults. It was a mournful spectacle."[28] Nor was this an isolated situation.

MORTALITY OF WORKERS

Dr. Holland of Sheffield oversaw a demographic investigation of the city of Leeds in 1842. The average age of death for the gentry, manufacturers, and their families was 44. For shopkeepers, it was 27 and for laborers, it was a terrifying 19! The aggregate average was 21, which demonstrates the preponderance of laborers in the population. Holland reported that, "We have no hesitation in asserting, that the sufferings of the working classes, and consequently the rate of mortality are greater now than in former times.

Indeed, in most manufacturing districts the rate of mortality in these classes is appalling to contemplate."[29] These specifics were increasingly well-known and the general trends were clear to the workers themselves. The source of their suffering in entrepreneurial neglect was equally apparent to the laboring classes.

The factory system represented a thoroughgoing transformation of industrial society. As a system of production, factories shifted the relations among masters, men and women to each other and to the means of production at least as much as it altered the process of manufacturing goods. These changes permitted an unprecedented level of economic growth. Britain was the first nation to be able to institute this unprecedented economic structure. The next chapter will demonstrate why Britain was able to achieve this feat of world historical significance.

5

WHY WAS BRITAIN FIRST?

The question of why Great Britain led the industrial revolution has been hotly debated ever since the eighteenth century, when the initial signs of modern industry emerged. Other countries clustered around the North Sea, notably France, the Netherlands and what became Belgium, had many of the same social, economic, and technological preconditions for industrialization—what made Britain unique? The answer to this question helps: (1) to explain why Britain was not able to maintain its economic supremacy, (2) to avoid assumptions about how to jumpstart industrialization that distort what entrepreneurs have done and can do, and (3) to understand how historical considerations can impact contemporary developmental policies in what is often termed the Third World.

PRECONDITIONS—COMPARATIVE ADVANTAGES

TRADE

Some of the reasons why Great Britain could initiate an industrial revolution have been discussed in earlier chapters. The extent of British foreign trade and the dependence of the British economy on this trade led to the development of a large corps of merchants. These entrepreneurs were essential to the growth of capital stock available for investment, to the creation of institutions that fostered trade, and to the acquisition and maturation of the Empire into a profitable endeavor. These merchants also played a vital role in integrating Britain into the emerging world economy. A consequence of Britain's expanding trade network was that products had to flow in both directions. To supply these products for trading purposes, a culture of entrepreneurship emerged to complement the increase in the number of merchants. Although relatively few merchants became industrial pioneers, the entrepreneurs who emerged to supply the needs of trade did turn to industrial development. Merchants also made marketability a primary consideration in product development. In this way, Britain's dependence on trade helped make the industrial revolution.

AGRICULTURE

The advanced state of agriculture in Britain also played an important role in fostering industrialization. Agriculture represented an enormous and continuing comparative advantage. At the dawn of the industrial age, the output per worker of British agriculture was one-third greater than France's and twice that of Russia, while Europe enjoyed double the productivity of any other part of the world. By 1851, British output per worker was twice that of any contemporary European state.[1] Not only did high agricultural productivity foster effective work habits throughout the population, but it also released labor. This labor could be employed in industry, but the path does not seem to have been direct. Instead, high wages or employment opportunities attracted rural labor to migrate to the "internal empire" of Ireland and Scotland, to the cities and abroad. This migration fostered urbanization and the growth of more sophisticated and dense markets that steadily increased demand for industrial products. In addition, agricultural productivity encouraged population growth which had a major impact on the growth of the market for manufactured goods. Current explanations for this agricultural productivity in Britain generally focus on the role of the state in fostering a system of land tenure based on a distinctive and inegalitarian system of property rights that increasingly favored the formation of more efficient, large estates.[2]

RESOURCES

The fertile soils that generously repaid the efforts of British farmers were a material resource of tremendous value. Lush grass fed sheep and other animals that provided both raw materials for industry and a better, more varied diet for the British people. Britain was also blessed with abundant sources of minerals including coal, copper, lead, tin, and iron. The quality of the ores was quite high, much more so than in France, Britain's greatest competitor. Not only did Britain have a more than adequate supply of mineral ores, they were also conveniently located. The three great coal fields—in Northumberland, Lancashire, and south Wales—are within a few miles of the North Sea, the Mersey estuary, and the Bristol channel respectively. The quality and quantity of these coal supplies, coupled with the relative shortage of wood, encouraged Britain to make the transition from organic to far more efficient inorganic (coal, water, and wind) sources of energy at least a half century before the rest of Europe. Early in the nineteenth century, England consumed 15 million tons of coal a year compared to 3 million tons for all of continental Europe combined.[3]

MINING

Britain also boasted other raw materials like kaolin clay deposits essential to the pottery industries as well as considerable limestone and slate deposits that were vital to its industrialization and urbanization. In 1854, mining employed more than 400,000 of whom half delved for coal. These men and women extracted raw materials worth about £40 million which represented about 6% of GNP. About 10% of domestic production of key minerals like iron and coal was exported.[4]

WATER TRANSPORT

As we shall see when we look at the role of the British navy, the island nature of the British state was a tremendous material resource. It was also a key to building an effective transportation network. Even without man-made improvements, nowhere in Britain is more than 70 miles from the sea and very few places are more than 30 miles from navigable water. The Severn and the Trent river systems provide water carriage to the industrial Midlands and the Thames and the Wash supply easy transport to major agricultural regions. In the seventeenth, eighteenth, and nineteenth centuries, the British state and entrepreneurs expended considerable capital on improving the waterways, building canals, and ensuring access to the rivers and streams as sources of industrial power. These efforts were not in any way unique to Britain; in fact, Britain was following in the wake of various continental countries in water transport. But because of the compactness of the island, the reach of the navigable rivers and the numerous ports, the improvements made to the British water system were more effective in creating a national transportation network and thus a national market than was possible in continental Europe.

Without question, the material advantages enjoyed by Britain contributed to industrialization. Once again, however, we must return to the issue of necessary versus sufficient conditions. These material advantages were neither necessary nor sufficient to industrialization. What matters most is what the British people did with these advantages. The rest of this chapter will focus on three (more or less well-known) unique attributes of Great Britain that were necessary to industrialization.

THE STATE, THE EMPIRE, AND THE ROYAL NAVY

COLONIAL TRADE

The Empire contributed enormously to the British industrial revolution. Thanks to the effectiveness of mercantilist trade policies like the Acts of Trade and the Navigation Acts, Britain profited more thoroughly from its expanding empire than rival European powers. An estimate of the scale of annual profit for the era leading up to the American Declaration of Independence in 1776 was £2.64 million out of an official total of British imports and exports from the colonies valued at £9.5 million (28%). The annual profits on the trade in human beings alone were equivalent to almost 40% of the sum total of all British commercial and industrial investment. Colonial trade comprised 15% of British commerce in the 1698 and one-third by 1774.[5] The protected colonial market for staple manufactured goods like woolens and for "new" products like cottons eased the rivalry between the two industries and facilitated a rapid and continued growth of exports. The new industrial goods went overwhelmingly to the colonies, thereby increasing demand and permitting continuous improvements in economies of scale. State regulation also suppressed potential competition in the thirteen American colonies in such key products as woolens and iron, diverting colonial manufacture to less profitable, less essential, supplemental areas. All colonial production was supposed to benefit the home country, but, of course, it did not always work that way.

SCOTLAND AND IRELAND

The ambivalence of mercantilism was most clear in Scotland and Ireland. Scotland was fully integrated into the British economy. Union in 1707 allowed the industries and mines of the region to develop and allowed impoverished Scots access to the English labor market. Scottish industry and commerce benefited disproportionately from its privileged access to the Empire. Ireland, however, was treated as a colony until 1801, although conditions improved after 1779 because British elites feared that events in North America would touch off a renewed crusade for independence. The Irish were encouraged to raise sheep and gather raw wool, but that wool could only be exported to England not used by Irish industry. This measure effectively destroyed the manufacture of woolens, which had been Ireland's greatest export. Throughout the eighteenth century and well into the nineteenth, efforts to develop Irish industry were crushed with deliberation. English goods were sold at a loss if necessary. Irish cattle, butter, and cheese were barred from the English market, but Ireland was not permitted to do the same to English goods. As compensation, Irish linen (whose manufacture was concentrated among the Protestants of Ulster) was protected and encouraged. It should not surprise, however, that such an unequal economic relationship led the Irish to become expert smugglers. Through conquest and mercantilism, the Hanoverian state created political conditions in Ireland and the rest of the Empire that greatly favored British manufactured goods. The scale and scope of this trade was vital to Britain's ability to inaugurate an industrial revolution.

THE NECESSARY BRITISH STATE

The second and perhaps the most vital attribute that was "necessary" for industrialization was the singular economic activities and political role of the

British state.[6] The government of Great Britain has the present-day reputation of being both more "democratic" and more "laissez-faire" than its competitors thanks to its institutions, notably the Parliamentary constitution, legal system, and an emphasis on individual enterprise. Thirty years of research has, however, revealed two startling conclusions. First, a number of other regions in Europe and even the maritime provinces of China and Japan enjoyed a surprising set of institutional resemblances to Great Britain that allowed them to also enjoy Smithian growth during the eighteenth century. Nor were the enormous benefits reaped by the British from their empire unique. What differed was the degree of protection (from both domestic and foreign challenges), stability, and order afforded by the British to its elites. This protection also took overtly economic forms: the British government fostered the creation of a relatively free domestic market for both production and consumption which unshackled innovation, allowed economies of scale, improved living standards, and assured profits.

A MILITARY STATE

The path that Great Britain forged to achieve an industrial revolution cannot be accurately portrayed without demonstrating the degree to which the British government achieved its aims through the application of military might. Many states rely on their military, but the breakthrough achieved by the British was that they managed to pay for their extraordinary level of military expenditures without either stifling growth or going bankrupt. Belying their "laissez-faire" reputation, the British were the most heavily taxed people on earth. From the Restoration to the end of Napoleonic wars, total tax revenue increased by a factor of seventeen while national income merely tripled. Most of this money went to pay for goods and services for the military. In that period, an astonishing 83% of such public expenditures were related to the military. Britain funded its wars through the expansion of the national debt. Before the Glorious Revolution of 1688, Britain's national debt was less than £2 million. By 1819, it had reached £854 million, which was 2.7 times of the total national income. Sixty percent of the taxes paid to the central government went to debt service. The ability of the British state to mobilize these phenomenal sums for war played an enormous part in British military successes during this crucial era.

NAVY

The cornerstone of British defense policy was investment in the Royal Navy. The building of an enormous fleet and its on-shore infrastructure were all dedicated to keep ships of the line at sea in strategic locations to act as the primary bastion of defense. The fleet also functioned as the guarantor of mercantilism: it protected British trade and the colonies, threatened enemy colonies and coastlines, and hunted merchant shipping—both hostile and neutral. By keeping out all seaborne invaders after 1688, Britain's maritime defense strategy bolstered trade, growth, and empire while helping to ensure internal stability.

LAND FORCES

Britain also dedicated enormous sums to hiring mercenaries from the German lands to fight its wars and to providing subsidies to countries willing to combat the designs of France and its allies. Only in a few rare cases were significant numbers of British troops committed to continental warfare. This strategy was more cost effective than maintaining large armies as its rivals were forced to do by the dictates of geography. Such an approach to defense policy permitted Great Britain to concentrate its armed forces on more remunerative pursuits: the conquest of new colonial territories and the assurance of domestic stability. The former required far less total expenditure than the latter. But overall, the British state spent 60% of its defense budget on various ground forces: its own, its allies, and on hired mercenaries.

INTERNAL ORDER

Regular regiments and various types of militias were all dedicated to preserving internal order. The effectiveness of these forces against potential invaders was doubtful at best. In considering why Britain was able to initiate the industrial revolution, however, it is crystal clear that defense against invasion was far less important than preventing subversion or rebellion in Scotland and Ireland or than protecting the existing social hierarchy and the network of property rights. The effectiveness of the navy as a defensive barrier enabled Britain to maintain a conspicuous military presence throughout the Isles and to employ exemplary displays of armed force whenever the status quo was threatened. Scots, Irish, workers, farm laborers, religious dissenters, political reformers, and the poor were all subject to thoroughgoing military rule whose oppressiveness increased over time to eliminate the unruliness of "an ungovernable people."

The recourse to force was particularly evident during the revolutionary and Napoleonic wars (1792–1815). The priorities of the British government were revealed by the fact that the Duke of Wellington began the Peninsular Campaign in 1808 with less than 10,000 troops, but in 1812, 12,000 troops were sent to stop the Luddites from breaking machines. At the same time, property owners were enrolled into a "patriotic" militia to confront the popular classes, the government made heavy-handed use of spies and informers, and 155 military barracks were constructed in industrial districts. As historian E.P. Thompson put it, "In 1816 the English people were held down by force."[7] Simply put, the British were able to industrialize first because they imposed *and the population tolerated* a degree of repression in defense of existing elites that none of its competitors could even dream of, much less imitate.

OTHER FORMS OF REPRESSION

British repression went far beyond the merely military; it was also political, legal, and economic. Whereas up to that time, England had enacted a greater degree of protection for individual and collective rights than most other European countries, paradoxically, in the age of the French Revolution and Napoleon, the average British person lost many of their customary rights and protections. Ostensibly passed to defeat the French challenge, new facets of legal repression inaugurated during that time included: Pitt's Two Acts of 1795 restricting individual liberties; the suspension of the Act of Habeas Corpus Act; and the 1797 Administering Unlawful Oaths Act. For workers, these years brought: the Combination Acts of 1799–1800 that prevented any sort of collective activity by laborers; the final abrogation of paternalist industrial legislation in woolens in 1809; the elimination of the power of officials to regulate wages that permitted employers to subject their workers to whatever conditions they cared to impose; and the repeal of the Elizabethan apprenticeship statutes in 1814. The transmutation of machine-breaking into a felony carrying the death penalty in 1811 demonstrates the impunity with which British elites utilized the legal system to protect their economic interests.

These new measures complemented long-standing legal and political means of intimidation and social control. Only a few need be mentioned: the religious settlement termed "Glorious" after 1688 disenfranchised Catholics, non-Anglican Protestants (dissenters) and all other faiths. Until 1832, those who did not accept the Church of England could not hold most offices, either local or national, and were excluded from the economic opportunities that could stem from access to the power structure. Those disadvantaged included most of the Irish and Scots peoples who became the most poorly paid and highly exploited groups of workers in Britain during the industrial revolution. The Corn Laws kept food prices artificially high to guarantee the profits of the landowning classes. At the same time, the high cost of living enforced a more industrious attitude to work on the part of laborers who would have preferred more leisure. Nor could skilled workers simply escape. To guard their productive advantages, the emigration of all machinists, not just those with unique or proprietary knowledge, was prohibited until 1824. As discussed earlier, the Poor Law encouraged both farming out unemployed workers and indenturing the children of the poor to industrialists.

OTHER INCENTIVES

The British state facilitated industrialization in other ways. Trade had been protected by the Navigation Acts since the mid-seventeenth century, but in 1784, Parliament enacted the "drawback": a bounty on the export of cotton goods paid for by taxation. It was later applied to other key industrial products. By stimulating exports, the British state guaranteed a certain level of sales and helped achieve economies of scale. Such a measure assisted both trade and industry. The same could be said for the numerous commercial treaties signed by Great Britain on highly advantageous terms in the eighteenth and nineteenth centuries. From Russia, to various Indian states, to Portugal, to Latin America, the British used their economic and naval power to force their way in and win either concessions or most favored nation trading status. The state chartered the Bank of England and enacted caps on interest rates to keep credit cheap and plentiful. Invention was stimulated by the establishment of patent protections and by support for certain key educational institutions that funneled private initiative in the most useful directions (see below). In sectors where Britain was not competitive, the state sponsored the illicit acquisition of needed workers or technologies. In addition, the British government assisted in the improvement of existing or the construction of new roads, ports, canals, and waterways. From this litany, it should be clear that contemporary estimates that only 0.5% of total public revenue was spent on "development" tells only part of the story.[8] Adam Smith's hope that the market would direct individuals in the most useful directions has been restated in a more accurate fashion by a number of present-day historians. They argue that the involvement of the British state in the economy should properly be known as "The Visible Hand."[9]

DOMINATION

Extensive legal, military, and political oppression had dramatic economic consequences. Given how dangerous and tightly disciplined the early factories were, the entrepreneurs of the early industrial revolution relied on apprentices, indentures, Irish, Scots, women, and children for a significant proportion of their labor force. It was not simply a matter of economy; it was also an expression of the domination of these groups by the elite. What requires emphasis is that those who went into the factory generally did so out of desperation or hunger. Higher wages were usually insufficient to convince these people to submit to factory life. Thanks to repression and a lack of other options, this domination of the working classes was widely accepted. The toleration by the working classes of a level of repression that would have sparked a revolution on the continent was the cornerstone of British labor discipline.

As British workers adapted to the time clock, new production methods, and the needs of the machine, entrepreneurs forged a greatly enhanced productivity to achieve an industrial revolution. Entrepreneurs knew that they could count on much deeper and much more systematic government support than on the continent.

It should not be forgotten that Karl Marx and Friedrich Engels based their analysis of the flaws of capitalism, in particular their argument that the profits of the current economic system came at the expense of enormous human suffering by the working classes, on their first-hand observation of British conditions. All European societies in the eighteenth and nineteenth centuries faced the same social, political, and religious pressures for reform, but British entrepreneurs could rely on the state to support their efforts to convince and/or force the working classes to supply the ever-growing demand for industrial products.

The Combination Acts

First passed by Parliament in 1799 and then amended in 1800, the Combination Acts followed hard on an Irish Rebellion in 1798, a naval mutiny, a poor harvest that led to high food prices, and continuing war with France. The Acts forbade associations of workers designed to raise wages, influence other workers, or affect working conditions. They remained in effect until 1824. The powerful response of the government to the request for help from the master millwrights made clear to manufacturers and workers exactly whose interests the state had foremost in mind.

Although the model for the Combination Act was a 1796 law that outlawed combinations of paper-workers, a petition of master millwrights received by the House of Commons on April 5, 1799, precipitated the first Combination Act. The petition read:

> that a dangerous Combination has for some Time existed amongst the Journeymen Millwrights . . . for enforcing a general Increase of their Wages, preventing the Employment of such Journeymen as refuse to join their Confederacy, and for other illegal Purposes, and frequent Conspiracies of this Sort have been set on Foot by the Journeymen, and the Masters have as often been obliged to submit, and that a Demand of a further Advance of Wages has recently been made, which not being complied with, the Men . . . have refused to work.

The response of the government headed by William Pitt the Younger was the Combination Act. As modified in 1800 (39&40 Geo. III, c. 100), it read:

> Be it therefore enacted that from and after the passing of this Act all contracts, covenants and agreements whatsoever . . . by or between any journeymen manufacturers or other workmen within this kingdom for obtaining an advance of wages, . . . or for lessening or altering their or any of their usual hours of time and working, or for decreasing the quantity of work . . . or for preventing or hindering any person or persons from employing whomsoever he, she or they shall think proper to employ . . .
>
> . . . every journeyman and workman who, after the passing of this Act, shall be guilty of any of the said offences . . . shall, by order of such Justices [Judges], be committed to and confined in the Common Gaol [jail] within his or their jurisdiction, for any time not exceeding three calendar months, or at the discretion of such justices shall be committed to some house of correction within the same jurisdiction, there to remain and to be kept to hard labour for any time not exceeding two calendar months.

Source: Hammond and Hammond, *The Town Labourer*, 100–101 and Cole and Filson, *British Working Class Movements*, 91–92.

SCIENCE, TECHNOLOGY, AND TINKERING

TECHNOLOGICAL CHANGE

British prowess at science, technology, and tinkering is the most commonly advanced reason for why Britain led the industrial revolution. In the eighteenth century, there was only a slight connection between science and technology. These two endeavors were practiced by different people for different purposes. In fact, despite Newton's great accomplishments, in basic science, Britain had no fundamental advantage. Only two of the five big breakthroughs of the period (termed macroinventions)—gas-lighting, the breast wheel, the Jacquard loom, chlorine bleaching, and ballooning—were British in origin.[10] The British state was also less involved in funding scientific research than their French rivals. However, science did have high prestige in Britain and scientific knowledge was more widely disseminated in Britain than on the continent.

CHEMISTRY

Even in areas where scientific theories were developing rapidly, it often took decades for a profitable practical application to emerge. In the late eighteenth century, chemistry shook off the associations with mysticism and alchemy that had shackled it for eons to emerge as a discipline whose principles were explored by rational scientific inquiry. Chemistry was also the first science to yield conspicuous, direct economic benefits. Several European governments as well as various manufacturers and merchants publicized their pressing needs for certain products and then provided the resources so that systematic investigations could be undertaken. A host of natural philosophers explored manufacturing problems ranging from how to make a more combustible gunpowder that did not smoke, to how to create new dyes for textiles, to bleaching white cloth. These attempts to satisfy the demand for chemical products influenced the practice of science. The researches of these budding chemists cemented an alliance among scientists, entrepreneurs and the state that led to faster and more startling advances in the nineteenth century.

ATOMS AND ELEMENTS

In 1774, English clergyman Joseph Priestley (1733–1804) determined that green plants consumed carbon dioxide and produced a gas that was necessary for something to burn. A French tax official Antoine Lavoisier (1743–1794) gave oxygen its name and began the process of categorizing the elements rationally in tabular form that was perfected by Russian Dmitry Medeleyev (1834–1907) only in 1869. John Dalton (1766–1844), a schoolteacher in Manchester, proposed a doctrine known as "atomism" in 1803. Experimentation with gases convinced him that elements were made up of "atoms," which he defined as indivisible. He also proposed that all substances were made up of varying proportions of elements. He devised a new system of chemical notation in equations (as in H_2O) and formulated laws to describe the ratios that helped to explain certain phenomena. Priestley's insight into the carbon cycle and Lavoisier's clarification of the relationships tying substances together plus Dalton's method of expressing these relationships gave rise to research into plants and animals at the molecular level. But initially, this chemical revolution had little direct practical application.

Inspired by Priestley, however, Swede Carl Scheele (1742–1786) identified chlorine in 1774. A decade later, Frenchman Claude-Louis Berthollet (1748–1822) discovered how to use chlorine as a bleaching agent. This breakthrough was taken up immediately by manufacturers all over western Europe despite the difficulties of using a gaseous element in an industrial process. As a professional scientist, Berthollet was not much interested in applying his discovery, but several of his students and nearby manufacturers of chemical products were. Some of these budding chemical entrepreneurs created a lab at Javel where chlorine was absorbed into an alkali to create "Javel water," a fairly effective means of bleaching cloth.

BLEACHING POWDER

In England, two Scots, Charles Tennant (1769–1838) and his partner Charles Macintosh (1768–1843) took out a series of patents regarding the use of chlorine that culminated in the formulation of bleaching powder in 1799. This powder, in which hydroxide or slaked lime is mixed with chlorine gas, is an effective, relatively inexpensive means of whitening cloth. Up to this time, cloth was left in an outdoor bleaching field where it was soaked in alkaline solutions and then exposed to air and sunlight before being treated with sour milk (and later sulfuric acid) to remove the excess alkali. This complicated, labor-intensive process could take up to 4 months. The addition of bleaching powder dissolved in water meant that the time spent in the bleaching fields was reduced to a few weeks and no additional labor was needed. Although Macintosh made the key breakthrough, Tennant squeezed him out of the patent application as well as the business they cofounded. Tennant went on to make a fortune from St. Rollox, his chemical works in Glasgow, the largest in the world at that time.

The search for an effective bleaching agent took decades to achieve and featured international cooperation amongst scientists and international rivalry amongst manufacturers. That it was Tennant who attained fame and fortune was not due to his unusual scientific or technological prowess. Rather his success stemmed from his sharp business practices, strict quality standards in manufacturing and successful protection from the British state. The length and continuing inconvenience of the bleaching process—which was not resolved until after the First World War—shows that science and technology cannot always fully meet demand as well as the gap between the theory and practice of chemistry.

MEETING OF THE MINDS

The state may not have supported research directly, but it did help to encourage interaction among scientists, laborers, and entrepreneurs in institutions like the Royal Society of Arts founded in London in 1754. Official sponsorship of the Royal Society helped to spur the formation of similar, but unofficial organizations also dedicated to scientific and technological issues like the renowned Lunar Society of Birmingham. This sort of imitation amplified the effectiveness of the state's endeavors. The "Lunatics" boasted members who were scientists like Joseph Priestley who first isolated the elements oxygen and nitrogen and who also identified hydrochloric and sulfuric acids. What helped make the Lunar Society such an important model was the close collaboration of someone like Priestley or Erasmus Darwin (father of Charles) with Matthew Boulton, James Watt, and Josiah Wedgwood, both in the laboratory and in the workshop. The high level of literacy, the great interest in science, and the relative wealth of the country also encouraged the publication of numerous pamphlets, journals, and books dedicated to scientific and technological concerns. These publications were seconded by numerous itinerant scientific lecturers who brought the spectacle of scientific experiments to the illiterate. These spectacles demonstrated concretely that the focus of most scientific teaching in Britain was to understand how things move—mechanics—which had an obvious benefit for those interested in machinery. As a result of these activities, British workers, especially the mechanics, had some understanding of basic scientific principles. This knowledge helped them to design, build, and maintain better, more effective machines. As Matthew Boulton put it, a skilled metal worker "can forge, file, turn and fit work mathematically true."[11]

SCIENTIFIC EDUCATION

Scientific education was a British strong suit. Literacy improved drastically in the age of Enlightenment: nearly half the men and over a quarter of the women were literate by the end of the eighteenth century. Much useful knowledge was not the province of the universities because of the limitations imposed by organized religion, but the universities did teach mathematics and support the advance of medicine. As a result, the best scientific training in England was found in the Dissenting Academies. Created because non-Anglicans refused to attend Church of England schools, these private institutions provided training in modern languages and practical mathematics to the middle and upper classes. Informal private salons and quasi-official academies devoted to specific issues also helped to spread the techniques of scientific agriculture and broadened the audience for scientific and techno-logical developments.

TINKERING

The practice of science and scientific education in Britain supported long-standing aptitude in technology and tinkering. It was here, not in basic science, that the British far surpassed their continental rivals. The British interest in tinkering was seen in the constant experimentation with how best to use coal as fuel, a process begun in the sixteenth century. The proper use of coal required skills that markedly improved British metallurgy and machine-building, which were among the best and most economical in Europe. This expertise was developed by artisans through decades of trial and error; it could not be passed easily to competitors and represented a major British advantage.

Charles Babbage (1791–1871)

Born in England, Babbage has become famous in recent years as the "Father of Computing" for designing an analytical machine that utilized the concept behind the Jacquard loom to create the basic design of the computer. A graduate of Cambridge University, Babbage held the Lucasian Chair of Mathematics there (Newton's old post). He founded the influential British Association for the Advancement of Science in 1832. A lifelong tinkerer and inventor, Babbage believed that precision engineering could best be achieved through the application of mathematical principles to industry. In this excerpt, he explains that good workmanship is essential to getting inventions to function.

In conducting experiments upon machinery, it is quite a mistake to suppose that any imperfect mechanical work is good enough for such a purpose. If the experiment is worth making, it ought to be tried with all the advantages of which the state of mechanical art admits; for an imperfect trial may cause an idea to be given up, which better workmanship might have proved to be practicable. On the other hand, when once the efficiency of a contrivance has been established, with good workmanship, it will be easy afterwards to ascertain the degree of perfection which will suffice for its due action. It is partly owing to *the imperfection of the original trials,* and partly to the gradual improvements in the art of making machinery, that many inventions which have been tried, and given up in one state of art, have at another period been eminently successful.

Source: Charles Babbage, *On the Economy of Machinery and Manufactures*, 4th ed. (New York: Augustus M. Kelley, 1971 [1835]), 264.

Different kinds of expertise were developed by British engineers, many of whom were self-taught, but who managed to design, plan, and implement some of the world's great human accomplishments such as the Britannia Bridge.

This revolutionary tubular bridge links the island of Anglesey to the mainland of Wales over the Menai Strait. The engineer, Robert Stephenson, was not permitted to block the strait with a conventional bridge for military reasons, so he used rectangular box sections of wrought iron to build a bridge that would still permit sailing ships to pass beneath it. It opened in 1850 and took three years to build. The Burndy Library, Cambridge, Massachusetts

As this bridge suggests, British engineers tended to specialize in larger machines and to be interested in big projects which also differentiated them from civil engineers on the continent.

IMPROVING ON THE WORK OF OTHERS

This same process of practical experimentation carried over to technological advances. British craftsmen excelled at taking other people's big ideas and tinkering with them until they could be applied profitably.

Tinkering produced a powerful stream of microinventions—developments that change a device or process incrementally rather than fundamentally—that, taken together, contributed enormously to the efficiency of machine-based production in Britain. Thanks to this marriage of theory and practice, Great Britain developed a unique scientific culture that generated a comparative advantage in microinventions. These microinventions were the basis of the effective utilization of technological breakthroughs that underlay both mechanization and the factory system. As part of this culture, specific skills and attitudes were fostered: British artisans were better at reading blueprints and using mock-ups to model how a large device should be built. These skills helped to focus the British on more practical machine designs that worked.

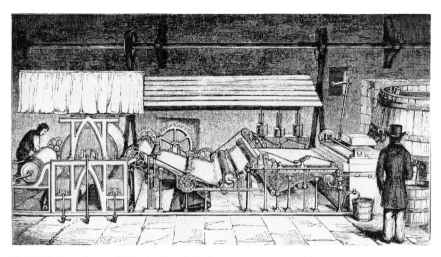

In 1799, Frenchman Nicholas-Louis Robert patented a machine that printed paper on continuous sheets. A British engineer, Bryan Donkin, improved the device greatly: it became known as the Fourdrinier machine after a London stationer who first adopted it in 1803. The Burndy Library, Cambridge, Massachusetts

Without this scientific culture, the industrial revolution would have taken a very different course.

MARKETING INNOVATION

The British also proved to be masters at taking advances in science and technology to develop new products to capture new markets. Product creativity by British entrepreneurs was essential to supplying the consumer demand unleashed by economic growth (see Chapter 8). This creativity went beyond variations on a theme. In a host of industries from pottery, to metalwork, to textiles, to glass, manufacturers embraced innovations in quality, product variety, and price as means of attracting the consumer. Taste and aesthetics were explored and cultivated through creative uses of publicity. Imitations of foreign (especially Asian and French) luxury goods were developed using British technological specialties. Lead glass crystal, porcelain, brassware, and silver plate were manufactured using artisanal expertise in metal alloys and newly developed machines to roll, stamp, and shape metals—all using coal as fuel. To create other products, totally new means of solving technical production problems had to be developed. For these industrial pioneers, there was a dynamic relationship between process innovation and product innovation. Some entrepreneurs created products that became and remain household names. The combination of innovation, imitation, publicity and marketing was a chief reason for British success in creating an industrial revolution because it married supply and demand.

Josiah Wedgwood (1730–1792)

Wedgwood was from a family of potters in Staffordshire. At the age of nine, he went to work for his brother in the family business and later served as his apprentice. When his brother refused to make him a partner, Josiah went to work for others. In 1759, he opened his own pottery works where he made the models and prepared the clay mixes in addition to running the operation. Wedgwood opened a new factory in 1769 near Stoke-on-Trent with partner Thomas Bentley that he named Etruria.

At first, Wedgwood specialized in simple, durable, everyday earthenware. His hearty cream-colored line was dubbed Queen's ware after Queen Charlotte who made him "Queen's potter." Wedgwood searched constantly for product innovation to combat the quality porcelain of Asia and the Royal Sèvres works in France. Declining sales of cream-ware led him to experiment with barium sulphate from which he produced jasper in 1773. This porcelain featured separately molded reliefs, usually in white. The use of other color schemes like black on red to imitate Greek vases required numerous trials and reliable kilns. As part of the experiments, Wedgwood invented a pyrometer to correctly measure kiln temperature. These experiments helped bring Wedgwood's scientific accomplishments to others including the Lunar Society which he joined. Other decorative themes taken from ancient Roman and Egyptian art made Wedgwood's goods into pieces of art; they were not just useful objects. But he also produced table china with whatever fad of the day seemed likely to sell.

Wedgwood was also an innovator in factory organization, marketing, and politics. He built a village for his workforce to live in. The village provided decent housing, but ownership of their housing gave Wedgwood enormous control over his workers' lives and those of their families. Machines were introduced to replace the potter's wheel, but it was in the division of labor and in industrial discipline that Wedgwood's advantage lay. In exchange for relatively high wages, he sought "to make such machines of the Men as cannot err," a strategy that helped to turn Staffordshire from a poor region of artisanal enterprises into a rich manufacturing district.

Wedgwood wooed royalty all over Europe. He sent expensive masterpieces both to them and to British ambassadors in their capitals, all prominently featuring his trademark. Beyond his hopes for patronage, he figured that the elite set the fashions for luxury goods and influenced taste. Then he sold imitations to the masses in Europe and North America at double the prices charged by his competitors. Another means of catching the public's eye was to establish a luxurious showroom first in London, then in other cities where the wealthy congregated. Traveling salesmen, another innovation for a manufacturer of luxury goods, blanketed England, the continent, the Empire, and the United States. His motto was that *"Fashion* is infinitely superior to *merit* . . . and it is plain from a thousand instances if you have a favourite child you wish the public to fondle and take notice of, you have only to make choice of proper sponcers."*

Finally, Wedgwood gathered together like-minded manufacturers to lobby the government for effective protection. A General Chamber of Manufacturers (1785–1787), of which Wedgwood was the most influential member, shaped the repressive Irish trade agreement of 1785. With regard to this "Irish blunder," he stated that, "We have already convinced the Minister of 16 capital errors in the arrangement, and he has now brought into the house [of parliament] a system so much altered, and with so many additions, that it may be called a new one."** The group also successfully pressured the government to reopen negotiations for even more favorable terms for British manufactures in a commercial treaty signed with France the following year. At his death, Wedgwood left a fortune of £500,000. His sons and nephew took over the business and Wedgwood products are still sold all over the globe.

* Cited by McKendrick, Brewer, and Plumb, *The Birth of a Consumer Society,* 100, 104, 105.
** From an undated letter, probably from June 1785 in Ann Finer and George Savage, eds., *The Selected Letters of Josiah Wedgwood* (New York: Born & Hawes, 1965), 283.

Britain was first. The sources of British leadership of an industrial revolution must be situated in a place and a time in order to understand what lessons can be drawn and what lessons must be avoided. Advanced agriculture, significant natural resources situated in accessible locations, and geography provided a useful base for development, but were not necessary preconditions of industrialization.

British reliance on trade became a strength: it facilitated the acquisition and expansion of an Empire that generated wealth, obtained markets, and guaranteed access to important raw materials. This wealth supported heavy taxes paid to the state that were used primarily for defense and the maintenance of law and order. In the British case, considerable defense monies were spent on the navy which had concrete mercantilist benefits, but far greater sums were spent on ensuring militarily that the position of British elites could not be challenged domestically. Entrepreneurs could count on the British state to support their attempts to discipline their labor forces, with violence if necessary. British entrepreneurs also proved extraordinarily capable at convincing enough people to accept the industrial order to allow the expansion of manufacturing without provoking a revolution. The success of the British state in defeating challenges both from within and from without were necessary to leadership of the industrial revolution.

Finally, British leadership was also predicated on science, technology, and tinkering, but not in the way that it is often thought. The British had no advantage in basic science and only held their own in achieving major technological breakthroughs. What British entrepreneurs did better than anyone else was to capitalize on technology through innovation and improvement. They changed how work was organized and acquired. They also developed new markets. Britain also had a considerable advantage in the mechanical knowledge and precision skills of its artisans. This knowledge and the scientific culture of Great Britain facilitated a stream of microinventions essential to the practical and economic application of scientific and technological advances. Without these key factors, an industrial revolution would probably have emerged somewhere, but their unique abilities in innovation and invention go a long way toward explaining why the British were the first to industrialize.

6

LEADS AND LAGS: COMPETING WITH A DOMINANT ECONOMIC POWER

As the first country to experience an industrial revolution, the British path to industrialization became the model for all who followed. Particularly in Great Britain and the United States, every nation that began the journey to industrial society in Britain's wake has been judged according to how closely they followed this model. Some countries like France have been portrayed as doomed to second-class economic status because they strayed from the path blazed by the British. Other nations like the United States and Germany whose economic development more closely resembled the British model are depicted as destined for success. This obsession with a unique set of geographical, cultural, economic, technological, and political circumstances has distorted present-day understandings of the conditions needed to industrialize. Kenneth Pomeranz, a historian of China, used the inability of the dominant Anglo-American understandings of the process of industrialization to explain events in other places to make an important assertion. He argues that all national experiences must be considered as deviations; none should be elevated to the status of the normative, no matter the timing or power of the economy in question.[1] Thus, despite the fact that the British led the way, those who wish to understand the applicability of their experience must recognize that a model has only limited applicability in successor economies. The very fact of a British industrial revolution changed the economic circumstances that others had to face. By looking at the challenges faced by entrepreneurs, government officials, and workers in other places, the multiple routes to an industrial society will be revealed. Rather than deviations, these paths should be considered as alternatives. These varied paths demonstrate the difficulties of rigidly applying an economic model and some of the economic consequences of the resultant policy errors.

The British initiated the industrial revolution in the late eighteenth century. They were, however, followed closely by their neighbors across the Channel—France and Belgium (the Austrian Netherlands)—in setting up the factory system and in industrial technology. It was politics that widened the gap between Great Britain and its rivals. As was crystal clear to contemporaries, the French Revolution in 1789 diverted continental resources into different channels and allowed Britain to capitalize on its strengths to achieve a universally recognized position of industrial dominance. This chapter explores how Britain's chief economic challengers dealt with their competitive disadvantages to achieve their own industrial revolutions. Despite concerted earlier efforts to foster industrialization, the next generation of industrial revolutions only began in 1815 and ran for approximately 50 years.

THE INDUSTRIALIZATION OF FRANCE

THE FRENCH REVOLUTION

The French recognized that something important was taking place in eighteenth-century Britain. Beginning around mid-century, a number of French policymakers and entrepreneurs influenced by the Physiocrats attempted to emulate those wellsprings of British industrial success that they lacked, namely elite domination and/or the cooptation of the working classes and encouraging working-class creativity and inventiveness. The French believed that even if they could not compete with the "First Industrial Nation," their fast rate of progress would allow them to compete with the British in the near term. This perspective on relative competitiveness helps to explain why the French agreed to sign a Commercial Treaty in 1786 that drastically lowered tariff rates. French efforts to imitate their island rival's approach to technological development, labor relations, entrepreneurialism, and mode of state involvement in the economy were brought to a screeching halt by the French Revolution.

MACHINE-BREAKING

The turbulent summer of 1789 witnessed an unprecedented wave of machine-breaking that was far more widespread and far more devastating than its better known, but far less significant English equivalent, the Luddites of 1811–1817. This machine-breaking was an important component of the political and social unrest that turned popular agitation into a Revolution. Machine-breaking in 1789–1791 was a visible sign that the French working classes would not go along with the hopes of entrepreneurs to inaugurate British-style industrialization. Pushed by invasion from abroad on every frontier, civil war and runaway inflation, working-class militancy accelerated during the Reign of Terror of 1793–1794 which led to about 50,000 deaths. This impressive level of popular mobilization and politicization was central to the French Revolution. Entrepreneurs feared "the threat from below"—it undermined their faith in their ability to implement or maintain the industrial discipline essential to the British model of industrialization. Although the new French regime struggled to continue and even advance their emulation of the

British economic model, the ongoing threat of violence forced key French leaders to recognize that if they trod in Britain's footsteps, a social revolution would break out. As a result of the political upheavals of the French Revolution, a new industrial path for France and for the rest of continental Europe had to be found and implemented.

CHAPTAL

Jean-Antoine Chaptal (1756–1832) was the architect of the French path to industrial society. A noted chemist and a wildly successful manufacturer of chemical products, Chaptal was Napoleon Bonaparte's most influential Minister of the Interior (1800–1804). It was thanks to his leadership that the French abandoned their plans to imitate the British and fashioned their own approach to industrial development. If the government played an essential role in British industrialization, on the continent, the demands imposed by being forced to play "catch up" compelled the state to take over many essential economic functions directly. The manner of state direction of the industrial economy inaugurated by Chaptal remained characteristic of the French industrial landscape throughout the nineteenth century and beyond.

Jean-Antoine Chaptal (1756–1832)

Born into a bourgeois family in Montpellier, Chaptal studied medicine and chemistry in Paris. His reputation in chemistry was based on solving practical problems. He wrote important treatises that detailed how to improve the production of wine, butter, and cheese that complemented his well-regarded chemical textbook and influential plans for educational reform. Ennobled in 1788, Chaptal was imprisoned during the Reign of Terror for his moderation. Late in 1793, he was released and charged with overseeing the production of gunpowder, a difficult task because of the lack of raw materials. Two years later, Chaptal returned to Montpellier to teach medicine before becoming professor of chemistry at the elite Paris Polytechnic in 1798. Under Bonaparte, Chaptal was named a councilor of state and charged with improving public education. Napoleon named Chaptal Minister of the Interior in 1800 where he remained until 1804. Upon leaving the ministry, Chaptal entered the Senate and was named Count of Chanteloup in 1808.

According to Chaptal, who built on Adam Smith's views, the nineteenth-century government's role in managing industry had three basic components. First of all, the state had to mend the damage done by the prerevolutionary administration. By depriving those involved in the production and distribution of goods of their proper place in society, the Bourbon regime had damaged French "public spirit" and alienated potential entrepreneurs. Only active state sponsorship of the social value of commerce and industry could repair centuries of contempt. Secondly, Chaptal asserted that, with regard to industry, "The actions of government ought to be limited to facilitating supplies, guaranteeing property, opening markets to manufactured goods and to leaving industry to enjoy a most profound liberty. One can rely on the producer to pay attention to all the rest." Yet Chaptal recognized that, in reality, the government could not be quite so "hands-off." To ensure that all French citizens could find gainful employment and to guarantee that the Revolutionary ideal of equality under the law existed in economic practice, the state must intervene. Chaptal contrasted the French emphasis on equality and its deep foundations in state efforts with Great Britain where "private interest directs all actions." To Chaptal, the public good required state mediation of the myriad of private interests.

Chaptal founded, revived or sponsored a host of institutions such as Chambers of Commerce, Consultative Chambers of Manufacturing, Arts and Crafts, industrial expositions, Councils of Agriculture, Arts, and Commerce and the Schools of Arts and Crafts, the Society for the Encouragement of the National Industry, the Museums of Arts and Crafts, and free spinning schools for women. This list is not exhaustive and demonstrates both Chaptal's commitment to state intervention in the economy and how wide open the field was for institutional innovation.

Chaptal was not just a bureaucrat or a theoretical chemist. He was also an entrepreneur. He created three large-scale chemical workshops around Paris. On his vast estate, he became vitally concerned—both scientifically and commercially—with improving the process of distilling sugar from grapes and naturalizing the sugar beet and merino sheep in France. In 1819, Louis XVIII named Chaptal a Peer of the realm. That same year, Chaptal published one of the first accounts of the nascent industrial revolution in France. For the rest of his life, Chaptal actively promoted educational reform to improve interaction between theoretical and applied science while employing his precepts to increase his personal fortune.

Sources: Jeff Horn, *The Path Not Taken: French Industrialization in the Age of Revolution 1750–1830* (Cambridge, MA: MIT Press, 2006) and Jean-Antoine Chaptal, *De l'industrie française*, ed., Louis Bergeron (Paris: Imprimerie nationale, 1993 [1832]).

A DIFFERENT APPROACH

The industrial policy fashioned by Chaptal and his collaborators and pursued by his successors was economically rational and market oriented. Without the same material advantages in coal, transportation, and geography, except in a few niche products, France could not compete in the key sectors of the British industrial revolution: cotton textiles, iron, and coal. For military reasons and to enable the growth of other, complementary sectors, the French spent enormous sums to achieve adequate expertise in iron smelting, cotton textiles, machine-building, and the use of coal as fuel. These efforts did not, however, succeed in challenging Britain's position for generations. This relative lack of success is not surprising: given France's endowment of natural resources and the available sources of energy, the British model of industrialization based on coal, iron, and cotton textile production as delineated by T. S. Ashton simply had less power to transform the national economy. French industrial success was predicated on discerning and supporting *other* products, *other* technologies, and *other* industries.

A Missed Opportunity

Chaptal laid solid foundations for long-term growth, but France missed a very real opportunity to become Europe's dominant economic power. Under Napoleon, France annexed northwestern and central Italy, the Rhineland, and Belgium (among other areas), which added 14 million more consumers for French producers, ominously lengthening the French demographic lead over Great Britain. These territories provided reservoirs of vital mechanical and/or technical knowledge in metallurgy, machine-building, and coal-mining. The established industrial centers of Piedmont, Lombardy, Belgium, and the Rhineland specialized in products and processes that complemented the needs of the French core in ways that presaged a promising synergy. These areas also contributed another form of human capital in their profusion of entrepreneurs, many of whom were accustomed to facing up to British competition and had experience in satisfying diverse groups of customers. Finally, the expanding frontier encompassed important reserves of raw materials that France had either lacked or had insufficient stocks of, notably Italian silk, Belgian coal and Rhenish iron. For 15 years, French borders closely resembled those of the original European Economic Community. In addition, through its satellites and allies, the French Continental System, in place from 1806 to 1813, linked Madrid to Warsaw, Copenhagen to Naples, and Amsterdam to Trieste. In this favorable atmosphere, French trade boomed as industry mechanized and modernized. Water-powered factories blossomed across the northern part of the country. François Richard, known as Richard-Lenoir, was the preeminent cotton manufacturer of Imperial France. He assured Napoleon that with the workforce under control and entrepreneurs encouraged, French industry could meet its competitive challenges. France could defeat Britain in the counting house and in the workshop as easily as it did on the battlefield, he asserted. Richard-Lenoir depicted the French industrial situation in simple yet evocative terms: "We have been born, but as children we cannot fight against grown men in the fullness of their strength, but in a few years we will be able to do so."[2] Where France had boasted only six large mechanized cotton mills in 1789, by 1814, there were 272. Since the output of machine-spun cotton yarn doubled between 1806 and 1808 and again (at a minimum) from 1808 to 1810, there was genuine cause for optimism.[3] Ultimately, Napoleonic overreaching in Spain and Russia doomed the Empire to defeat by a grand coalition of European powers, but, in the first decade of the nineteenth century, the French threat to British industrial hegemony was very real.

THE SPREAD OF KNOWLEDGE

To catch up with Great Britain and to develop or protect productive specialties, the French needed to acquire and spread technical knowledge. Although financial incentives for innovation and the enticement of skilled workers from abroad played important roles in this process, education was at the heart of the long-term French approach to becoming competitive. Educational institutions were to facilitate the application of French predominance in basic science, especially in chemistry, mathematics, and medicine to the problems of production. French education also aimed to spread mechanical knowledge more widely and deeply among the laboring classes. These educational efforts began during the Revolution with the creation of the National Institute and the Polytechnique in 1794 which were staffed by some of the best scientific minds alive. These elite institutions were supposed to provide expert training and to reorient theoretically minded French elites toward practical problems of industry and engineering. It was hoped that their effects would trickle down the French educational system. Thanks to Chaptal, students at specialized training schools for mining and civil engineers also began to spend part of each year in the field learning about the practical problems they would someday face. The thorough reform of the university system undertaken by Napoleon in 1808 supported these goals. To bridge the gap between the elite and the rest of the population, the French opened two Schools of Arts and Crafts (1803, 1811) where skilled workers, foremen, engineers, and scientists melded scientific theory and hands-on practice with machines. According to its founding statutes, these schools were to "train petty officers for industry."

INSTITUTIONS

Chaptal and his collaborators also sought to institutionalize the type of interaction of scientists, innovators, entrepreneurs, and bureaucrats that took place in the London Society of Arts and the Lunar Society of Birmingham. Councils of agriculture, manual arts, and commerce were established in each department in 1801. Chambers of Commerce were revived in large cities in 1802 and 150 Consultative Chambers for Manufacturing, Arts and Crafts were founded in 1803 to ensure that people in small and medium-sized urban areas had access to technical knowledge and learned of market opportunities. Other institutions that complemented these efforts included the Society for the Encouragement of the National Industry created in 1801 (see insert), the Museums of Arts and Crafts, the Conservatory of Arts and Crafts in Paris, as well as the local and national industrial expositions inaugurated in 1798 (see Chapter 8). Widening the net even further, in 1833, France mandated the creation of an elementary school in every canton. The teacher was salaried out of local tax revenue. This was the first step toward universal primary education.

The Society for the Encouragement of National Industry

This quasi-public, but officially private organization was founded in 1801 with the strong support of Chaptal. Many other highly placed government officials were among the initial 300 members. Joseph-Marie de Gérando, a member of the National Institute and the long-time Secretary-General of the Minister of the Interior, explained its function at the inaugural meeting in January 1802.

> Without question, the best means of favoring the development of industry are to improve [technical] knowledge, to release people from the shackles of routine and to employ inventions to their best advantage. However, to enlighten those concerned, it is necessary to unite them and have them associate with each other and with the learned and thus to form an alliance between theory and practice.

The group's intent was to bring together "officials, scientists, merchants, manufacturers, artisans and inventors" in order to "excite emulation, spread knowledge and support talent." To accomplish these goals, the society endorsed the following methods in their governing statutes of 1804.

1. Distributing models, designs, or descriptions of new inventions.
2. Creating written instructions for useful and little-known processes.
3. Experiments and demonstrations to judge new methods which will be announced and published.
4. Reimbursements, advances, and encouragements to meritorious *artistes*.
5. Publication of a *Bulletin* distributed only to members containing the deliberations of the Society, its correspondence and announcing discoveries made in France or abroad.
6. The distribution of prizes.

These activities were supported by an annual subscription of 36 francs and supplemented by subsidies from the Ministry of the Interior as well as by generous personal donations from Chaptal among others. The society contributed to a number of French technological advances and improved techniques with signal successes in the perfection of the Jacquard loom for silks in 1808 and the naturalization of the sugar beet. Later recipients of funds from the Society included Pasteur, Beau de Rochas and the Lumière brothers.

Sources: Discours prononcé par le Citoyen Degerando, de l'Institut National et Membre du Conseil-général d'Agriculture, Arts et Commerce du ministre de l'Intérieure, à la Séance d'ouverature (October 31, 1801) and Jean Pigeire, *La vie et oeuvre de Chaptal* (Paris: doctoral thesis, 1931), 399–400. Translations by Jeff Horn.

INVENTION

Taken together, these educational and institutional efforts encouraged the French to develop and diffuse technical knowledge and to compete with the British. From such late eighteenth-century innovations as ballooning (1784), chlorine bleaching (1784), and the pencil (1798), during the Napoleonic era,

Joseph-Marie Jacquard, a silk mill owner in Lyon, recognized that weaving was the bottleneck in the production process. His loom, first developed in 1801 and improved in 1808, used pasteboard cards to direct the rods imprinting a pattern that could be repeated. The Burndy Library, Cambridge, Massachusetts

the French moved on to more useful and more practical inventions such as the Jacquard loom, new cotton-printing machines and a means of spinning flax. Once the battle of Waterloo ended the dream of Empire, the stream of macroinventions dwindled, but, as a result of the initiatives taken by Chaptal and his collaborators, the institutions discussed above fostered a flood of microinventions that played a major role first in maintaining and then in improving French industrial competitiveness.

A DIFFERENT MODEL

France industrialized thanks to several internationally competitive sectors. These sectors spanned a wide variety of luxury goods including silk textiles. France also earned profits by selling its cottons, woolens and other products to less advanced economies.

Although France developed its fair share of factories, the factory system had less influence in the industrial economy. France was also far more dependent on water power than its European competitors. Instead, artisanal production, based on fashion, taste, and craftsmanship remained a far more important part of the economy than across the Channel. This approach to industrialization

With a nearly endless stream of microinventions, French inventiveness permitted the creation of new designs and new patterns for textiles. This
example of a fashionable cotton calico, which incorporates four different
types of mechanical stitching, was originally dyed a brilliant mauve. It was
fabricated in 1833 by Koechlin Brothers. The Burndy Library, Cambridge,
Massachusetts

has been termed "flexible specialization" and is now understood as a viable
alternative developmental approach to the British pathway.[4]

GROWTH

France's position as an industrial follower should not obscure its significant economic successes. Despite a clearly inferior economic and political
position, French industry grew relatively rapidly in the period 1815–1850.
Growth spurted in the 1850s thanks to the newly constructed railroad network. Estimates of industrial expansion for the period range from 2.5% to
3.4%. Agricultural growth was also strong at 1.2% annually in the half century
from 1820 to 1870. Over the long term, France averaged a 1.4% annual increase in per capita economic growth between 1815 and the outbreak of the
Great War in 1914.[5] In the century from Waterloo to the First World War,
on a per capita basis, French economic performance was broadly comparable to that of Great Britain. British per capita income remained higher—by
about 20%—but the gap between Britain and France did not widen even at
the height of British industrial dominance in the first half of the nineteenth
century.[6] France enjoyed impressive long-term growth, both overall and per
capita, particularly in light of its slower population expansion and smaller
colonial empire.

French society and its structures changed dramatically as a result of industrialization during this period. France had an industrial revolution, albeit
one more gradual and less abrupt than Great Britain's, much less than the

other follower economies. If, under Chaptal's stewardship, French short-term industrial performance did not quite equal Great Britain's, that is understandable given the limitations in French factor endowments, the growth of the domestic market, imperial advantages, capital stock, and the transport system. It is a measure of growing French competitiveness that, by 1860, they were once again willing to sign a commercial agreement bordering on free trade with Britain, then at the height of its industrial dominance.

THE SPREAD OF INDUSTRIALIZATION TO NORTH AMERICA

THE AMERICAN REVOLUTION

The seeds of the industrial revolution in North America were laid down during the Revolutionary war of 1775–1783. Separation from Britain meant that the thirteen colonies were cut off from the British Atlantic system. A naval blockade barricaded the former colonies from their long-time markets and suppliers. American artisans and manufacturers stepped in to fill the gaps, but it took two generations for Americans to build up an infrastructure capable of supporting the first steps toward industrialization. A further two generations passed before the United States produced manufactured products that could compete on the world market. However, given its phenomenal material advantages in land, agricultural products, timber, iron, coal, and other ores, the United States was a potential economic superpower, but even after the industrial revolution, that vast potential was only beginning to be realized.

Current commentators focus on four chief factors in stimulating American industrialization. The U.S. government played an important role in protecting emerging industries through the tariff, in establishing legal protections such as patent rights, in funding or enabling internal improvements in transportation and other facilities, and in supporting technical innovation. Secondly, the United States shared fully in the British consumer revolution of the eighteenth century. Based on their prior experience as British subjects, the nascent nation demanded all kinds of goods. Powerful consumer demand accelerated over time as American wealth grew and the phenomenal natural resources of the continent were harnessed. This growing consumer demand was identified and catered to by a host of imaginative entrepreneurs who initiated a managerial revolution in both small and large-scale manufactures that set the stage for innovative production processes. In developmental terms, this third factor was akin to skipping rungs on the industrial ladder. Finally, although a great deal of American exports stemmed from plantation agriculture worked by slaves, slavery is generally understood to hinder industrial development. The free labor of the northern, middle

Atlantic and western states, which enjoyed extraordinary opportunities for physical mobility and economic advancement, produced goods that absorbed a significant proportion of the enormous export earnings of the southern states, thereby preserving that wealth for the new nation. This synergy was vital to U.S. economic development. These aspects of the American economic structure shaped and quickened the industrial revolution in the United States.

YANKEE INGENUITY

The inhabitants of North America made their own tools. Their geographical isolation and the immaturity of the fractured regional markets left them little choice. As a result, many Americans were more familiar with the workings of significant, practical technologies such as mill works than their European cousins. On the plus side, where it was necessary, as in the precision work that went into making the gunlock for a Pennsylvania rifle or a clock's gears, Americans were able to use traditional craft techniques to supply what was needed. An intense and long-lasting shortage of skilled labor also meant that American artisans, both before and after independence, had to make a wide variety of products. The lack of incentives to specialize made American mechanics more flexible and more open to innovation, but it also meant that they were not always as skilled in performing certain tasks. The relative dearth of workers was accentuated by the attraction of the frontier; in the United States, labor-saving machinery was not just a means of increasing profit, it was a necessity. Particularly in New England and the Middle Atlantic states, the myriad fast-running streams were soon harnessed to the needs of industry. In combination with the nearly inexhaustible supply of wood, the widespread availability of water to power machines retarded both the iron and coal components of British-style industrialization. Long after independence, the United States still did not smelt iron with coke. American manufactures were not of high quality nor were they able to compete with equivalent European products, in part, because of matters of taste (see Chapter 8) but also, in part, because demand was so overwhelming that quality was less of a consideration. These labor and geographical conditions strongly impacted the nature and timing of industrialization in the United States.

TECHNOLOGY TRANSFER

During its industrial revolution, the United States was a major international importer of technology. The United States did boast several noted inventors and scientists like Benjamin Franklin, Thomas Jefferson, Joseph Priestley (who immigrated in 1794), and Eli Whitney and developed a few important innovations during the eighteenth century like the Pennsylvania rifle, the Conestoga wagon, and an improved axe along with the cotton gin. Despite these promising signs, the United States relied on others for its industrial technology. Most of the inflow of technology came from Great Britain and much of it was illicit because of British prohibitions on the export of machines and machinists. For example, Samuel Slater, who brought the Arkwright system of factory production to the United States, was able to leave Great Britain only by posing as a farmer (see Chapters 4 and 5). After the end of the War of 1812, however, the pace of American innovation, at least in textiles, picked up markedly.

WALTHAM SYSTEM

Boston merchant Francis Cabot Lowell (1775–1817) played a key role in American industrialization. During a two-year trip to England, he, like Slater before him, attempted to memorize the design of an important textile machine in the factories he visited, in this case, the power loom. When he returned to the United States, he and mechanic Paul Moody reconstructed the machines, adapting them to the materials available. With a new textile machine ready to put to use, Lowell and a group of partners created the Boston Manufacturing Company in 1813 to supply the demand that had accumulated because of the wartime blockade by Great Britain. As with many European enterprises, they raised capital by selling shares—the firm was ultimately capitalized at an impressive $600,000. These merchants sold shares mostly to their friends, relations, and business acquaintances, but the model of a joint-stock or shareholder corporation rapidly became widespread in American business (self-financing by ploughing back profits was, however, vital in sectors with fewer capital requirements than textiles).

The new company chose a site along the Charles River in Waltham, Massachusetts. In a brand-new brick building, Lowell harnessed water power to mechanize the conversion of raw cotton into cloth. Although given credit in the United States for being the first to integrate the entire process in a single structure, the British, French, Belgians, and Prussians had created such mills for a generation. The formation of an integrated firm was significant, however, because it abandoned New England's long-standing reliance on domestic manufacture. Waltham's corporate structure and management practices became a model for other American factories, especially when the coarse cotton cloth they made sold well.

Nearly the mill's entire labor force of 300 was composed of girls fresh from the farm. The girls, some as young as 15, received much lower wages than men, but they could live in company boardinghouses that were clean and respectable—they even had official chaperones! For these girls, the factory was a way off the farm and a means of engaging in religious and educational

Samuel Slater (1768–1835)

Born in England to a wealthy family, Slater was apprenticed to Jedediah Strutt, one of Richard Arkwright's partners. From Strutt, one of the largest textile manufacturers in Britain, he learned both management and the technical side of manufacturing. In 1789, he finished his apprenticeship which included a stint as a mill supervisor and decided to emigrate to the United States. He was drawn by the hefty bounties offered by several American states to anyone who could bring or build the latest model cotton textile machines. Slater came first to New York, but he was disgusted by the machines and organization of the group that offered the bounty. Instead, he moved to Pawtucket, Rhode Island, to work with Quaker merchant Moses Brown who had employed a number of skilled workmen and constructed several prototype machines.

Slater rejected the existing designs. Instead, from memory, he drew up plans for the Arkwright carding machine and spinning frame and then had the craftsmen assembled by Brown build the machines. The mill began operation in 1790 with workers walking on treadmills to power the machines; the following year, this plant became the first U.S. factory to produce cotton yarn with water-powered machinery. It operated on the British pattern: 12 hours a day, 6 days a week with a heavy complement of child laborers aged 7 to 12 who worked for very low wages. Slater became a partner, but soon formed another firm that built a separate mill in Pawtucket. Both mills made yarn which was sold to weavers. These enterprises benefited from the embargo on British goods imposed in 1807 that enabled Americans to replace temporarily the British in many domestic markets. Later, Slater founded a number of other mills for both cotton and wool scattered around New England, including one at the modestly named Slatersville (now part of North Smithfield), Rhode Island. These "integrated" water-powered mills contained both spinning and weaving operations within the same factory building and became quite widespread after 1815.

Slater's approach to finding and disciplining labor was deeply paternalistic. Once on his own, he employed young, unmarried women and recent immigrants. At Slatersville, families lived and worked in the community surrounding the mill. Tenement houses, a store, and even a Sunday school (the first in the United States) were provided for the workforce by the company. In the aftermath of the 1829 downturn, however, Slater lost control of several of his mills. To restore his fortune, Slater increasingly focused on finding competitive advantages and then maximizing profit. Accomplishing these goals led Slater and his sons to loosen the grip of paternalist control over the labor force in hopes of exhorting them to greater efficiency.

Slater took advantage of government incentives and tariff protection plus the capital of Quaker merchants as well as the machine-making skills of Yankee artisans along with the strong work habits of the labor force to become one of the most successful men in New England. When the business environment became rockier, his managerial practice evolved to become more efficient. Known as "the Father of the American Industrial Revolution," Slater, like Arkwright and Strutt, his models, was not a technical innovator; rather he was an economic opportunist whose most important expertise was in management where he became the model for a new, more capitalistic businessman.

Sources: Brooke Hindle and Steven Lubar, *Engines of Change: The American Industrial Revolution 1790–1860* (Washington, DC: Smithsonian Institute Press, 1986), 61–65, Jonathan Prude, *The Coming of Industrial Order: Town and Factory Life in Rural Massachusetts, 1810–1860* (Amherst: University of Massachusetts Press, 1983), 34–64, and Barbara Tucker and Kenneth Tucker Jr., "The Limits of *Homo Economicus*: An Appraisal of Early American Entrepreneurship," *Journal of the Early Republic* 24 (Summer 2004), 208–18.

activities, all while earning cash wages. The boardinghouses enabled these girls to abandon part-time agricultural work: they were now industrial workers. These women and their employers were influenced by the religious revival known as the "Second Great Awakening" that made discipline seem more necessary to the entrepreneur and more acceptable to the workers. Enough Waltham-type mills were constructed that finding sufficient girls to staff the factories became difficult. The original Waltham mill though had little difficulty attracting and keeping a loyal workforce.

Lowell himself died young, but the system he created paid extremely high profits. When the Boston Manufacturing Company expanded and created its own mill town in 1822 along the Merrimack River, they named it after him. The company chose a site with a 30-foot waterfall that could accommodate the largest waterwheels in North America; they were capable of running in any season and in any weather. Ultimately, the industrial city of Lowell housed 20 mills and 6,000 workers (5,100 of whom were women aged 15–29). By the end of the 1820s, ten of the largest corporations in the United States made use of the hydraulic system established in Lowell.[7] In 1850, 20% of all U.S. cotton cloth was made there.

For a generation, the directors maintained a highly regulated and highly profitable community and mill complex. The machinery was continually improved and replaced thanks to the efforts of tinkering managers, engineers and workers. Bezaleel Taft described the rapid technological obsolescence of textile machines in 1832:

the use of expensive and well-constructed machinery has been entirely superseded by the introduction of new improvements, by which a savings in labour was to be obtained beyond the value of the old machinery, or the expense of the new. In this way, the garrets and outhouses of most of our manufactures have been crowded with discarded machinery, to make room for that of more approved character.[8]

Effective management spurred this constant improvement. Such changeover was far more common in the United States than in Europe where profitable modes of production were updated only as a last necessity rather than as a matter of course.

When not at work (13 hours a day), the young women of Lowell, like their Waltham progenitors, lived in dormitories, separated from their families, where they were subject to "moral instruction" including the requirement to "attend public worship ... and to conform strictly to the rules of the Sabbath." They were also to keep clean, while avoiding both "ardent spirits" and "frivolous and useless conversation." This heavy-handed managerial paternalism was a way of combating social opposition to women working outside the home and of attracting laborers, but the positive social aspects and relatively high pay lasted only as long as the good times. When a sharp downturn hit in the mid-1830s, Lowell's vaunted mills also experienced labor problems when management tried to cut wages by a quarter.[9] Despite the ambivalent aspects of the managerial practice of Lowell and the mills in Lowell, these innovations in management and factory organization were the seed of what became known as the American system of production.

THE LIMITATIONS OF EARLY INDUSTRIALIZATION

The creativeness of entrepreneurs like Slater and Lowell have been given enormous attention by historians and economists. It is no accident that the American Museum of Textile History is located in Lowell, Massachusetts. These entrepreneurs and their activities have entered the lore of an inevitable and transcendent American economic development, but their impact has been strongly overstated. Despite dramatic increases in the volume of production from 46,000 yards of cotton cloth in 1805 to almost 142,000,000 yards 25 years later, these textiles producers could not even satisfy the American market. As the U.S. population grew (from 4 to 13 million between 1790 and 1830), roughly equivalent to that of England and Wales (14 million in 1830), supply failed to equal demand. European, especially British and French textiles continued to flow into the United States despite the costs added by the tariff and shipping.[10] In fact, only a relatively high tariff kept a significant percentage of domestic sales for American producers. According to contemporary estimates, in 1846, the United States boasted 2.5 million spindles for cotton (2.25 million in the Northeast), not quite 9% of the world total whereas Great Britain had more than 60% and France had nearly 15%.[11] In textiles, Americans innovated, but were not yet competitive.

ARMORY PRACTICE

U.S. international competitiveness was most apparent in any product that required machine tools. The federal government inadvertently fostered American specialization in machine tools and precision production. Around 1800, following the French example, the federal armory at Springfield, Massachusetts, began to break down the tasks that went into the manufacture of guns. This division of labor proceeded rapidly. By 1815, thirty-six separate tasks had been identified and, by 1825, about a hundred. In 1855, there were more than 400 different operations involved in making a gun with interchangeable parts at the Springfield armory. Production reached 20,000–30,000 muskets annually in the 1840s, and, at the height of the Civil War, the Springfield Armory produced a mind-boggling 276,000 muskets in a single year.[12] As in Europe, workers did not like to see their skills discounted. Nor did they appreciate the labor discipline that the managers of the armory insisted on. Worker resistance was, however, successfully overcome in the 1820s and 1830s. Thanks to the armory's example, the factory discipline developed at such cost in Great Britain became standard operating procedure in the machine shops of New England relatively easily.

If the division of labor was one key to armory production, mechanization was its twin. Over the course of 35 years, mechanics adapted or invented special-purpose machines to produce precision parts either in wood or metal. These machines undermined the influence of skilled workers to allow labor cost savings and permitted greater quality control. Mechanization was possible because of the general familiarity of Americans with machines. An official visiting the Springfield armory in 1841 commented:

the skill of the armorer is but little needed: his "occupation's gone." A boy does just as well as a man. Indeed, from possessing greater activity of body, he does better.

The difficulty of finding good armorers no longer exists; they abound in every machine shop and manufactory throughout the country. The skill of the eye and the hand, acquired by practice alone, is no longer indispensable; and if every operative were at once discharged from the Springfield armory, their places could be supplied with competent hands within a week.[13]

Thanks to the federal government's willingness to pay a premium for weapons with interchangeable parts, and the introduction of inspectors to insure that only correctly made parts were used, machine tools were invented, improved, and used to manufacture a wide variety of parts. Although the weapons made at the Springfield and Harpers Ferry, Virginia, armories were more expensive than those without interchangeable parts, the federal government accepted the added cost. At the same time, federal superintendents fostered a different attitude toward the work process, division of labor, and mechanization that, taken together, was called "armory practice." These production methods, like the acceptance of factory discipline, spread from the armories to other machine shops throughout the country and then to the manufacture of other products. Armory practice was the other essential foundation of the American system of production, although not of true mass production, which only became possible thanks to a new wave of technological developments at the tail end of the nineteenth century.

INVENTION

American facility with tools and the persistent shortages of labor, both skilled and unskilled, inspired tinkering and invention. The number of patents is a very rough (and somewhat problematic) approximation of the interest in new ways of doing things. By this gauge, invention increased markedly with the embargo on British goods in 1807 and accelerated greatly in two spurts, one in the mid-1820s and another in the late 1840s. Many early patents concerned improvements to existing devices such as the lightning rod or the steamboat, while others were American technological implementations of scientific advances from abroad. An example of the latter is Samuel Morse's telegraph. Patented in 1840 after 8 years of development, this device was developed concurrently by Charles Wheatstone in Britain (among others) and was based on the advances in electromagnetism of French scientist André-Marie Ampère (1775–1836). Morse's system got a trial run thanks to a $30,000 grant from Congress in 1843 to construct a telegraph line between Baltimore and Washington. The successful trial run the following year helped Morse and his partners dominate the emerging telegraph industry.[14] Other successful patents were based on incremental improvements as with Isaac Merritt Singer's (1811–1875) sewing machine that added the foot treadle in 1851 to the lock stitch machine patented in 1846. By replacing hand stitching, the first sewing machines afforded at least a 500% increase in productivity. The production of Singer Sewing Machines grew from 2,200 units in 1853 to half a million in 1870.

The burgeoning commercial success of American inventions in the middle third of the nineteenth century, generally based on precision metalwork or machine tools, spurred the American industrial revolution.

STEAMBOATS

If Robert Fulton's paddle-wheeled steamboat *Clermont* voyage from New York City to Albany in 1807 inaugurated steam travel in the United States, the new era in transportation was part of a broader phenomenon.

Soon steamboats traveled regular routes on the Hudson, Delaware, James, Susquehanna, Ohio, Missouri, and Mississippi Rivers (among many others) as well as their tributaries and the Great Lakes. Thirteen years after Fulton's feat, the number of steamboats plying the Ohio and Mississippi river systems reached 69; it rose to 187 in 1830 and 536 in 1850. Not only could steamboats go upriver far more easily, but by the mid-1820s, they could also travel up to 100 miles a day, whereas other boats could achieve 20 miles only under good conditions. The emergence of steamboats also helped to spread knowledge of engines and precision metallurgy especially along the Ohio River and its tributaries. In Pittsburgh, Wheeling, Cincinnati, and Louisville, industrial development followed in the wake of this knowledge.[15]

The new sewing machine demonstrated American technological prowess, but it was in marketing that Singer beat his competition most handily. The Burndy Library, Cambridge, Massachusetts

Fulton's *Clermont* (1807). The commercial success of this ship began a revolution in transportation that increasingly tied all the world's rivers into the world economy. The Burndy Library, Cambridge, Massachusetts

CANALS

Canals complemented steamboats to link distant parts of the far-flung nation. The most notable of the large number of canals built during this era was the Erie Canal financed by the state of New York. Stretching 363 miles, the canal was completed in 1825. By joining the Hudson River and Lake Erie, the so-called Eighth Wonder of the World crossed the Appalachian Mountains to link the port of New York with markets hundreds of miles in the interior and vice-versa. Because of the expense of building and maintaining canals, the vast distances to be traversed, the limited tax revenues of local and state governments in the United States, and the emergence of the railroad as a transportation rival, less than 3,400 miles of canals were built during the era of the industrial revolution. Canals linked several key hubs like the Great Lakes and the river systems of the Midwest, but the exorbitant cost of building—an average of $37,580 per mile—ensured the dominance of railroad.[16]

THE RAILROAD

If steamboats and canals boosted the market access of vast sections of the continent, the railroad generalized this process by expanding the area of land

John Stevens' locomotive was the first to be made in America. From humble technological beginnings, the railroad played a central role in creating a world economy. The Burndy Library, Cambridge, Massachusetts

that could be profitably exploited almost to infinity. The railroad emerged as a viable technology around 1815 due to the constant improvement of the high-pressure steam engine by British engineers. Based on this technological advance, a steam locomotive traveled from Liverpool to Manchester in 1830 at the unprecedented speed of 16 miles an hour. The enormous financial success of this line spawned imitators and encouraged governments to support railroad building. From the start, U.S. companies bought British engines, but they had to be adapted to American conditions.

Completed in 1833, the Camden and Amboy railroad linked New York and Philadelphia to become the first working line in North America. Given a monopoly by the state of New Jersey, this railroad company became one of the largest corporations in the United States. The cost of building the lines was significantly cheaper than in England or in Europe, but the returns were proportionately vast.

The enormous transport needs of the United States found their outlet in the "Iron Horse." By 1865, thanks to the support of various states and the federal government as well as the initiative of private citizens, the United States had 35,000 miles of railroad track, 3.5 times that of the United Kingdom. Yet the 10,000 miles of British track constituted a dense web; this was not the case in the United States. For Americans, because of the regional concentration of industry and the reliance on water power, the railroad was often the first tangible sign of the industrial revolution. Great Britain and the United States led the way in building railroads, but by 1870, extensive railroad systems crisscrossed most of the continent of Europe and the British colonies of Canada, Australia, and especially India, boasted their own networks.

In the United States and other follower industrial nations, railroads as well as the other "internal improvements" had particularly powerful economic and social effects. By lowering the cost of transporting heavy goods, increasingly remote areas became part of the global economy. Manufactured goods and raw materials flowed much more easily, rapidly, and, most importantly, much more cheaply than ever before. Before the railroad, the paper industry of western Massachusetts paid 8–24 cents per ton-mile to get their goods to market. In 1865, their freight charges had dropped to 4.5 cents per ton mile and with the growing speed and ease of access, they no longer had to maintain large inventories in their sales depots.[17] With markets widening and costs falling, larger and larger factories could be built, allowing greater and greater potential profits. The ease and relative affordability of transportation meant that industrial production now could be moved away from the sources of raw materials. As a result, cities boomed at an accelerated pace.

THE GOVERNMENT'S ROLE

As in Great Britain and France, the government encouraged industrial growth via tariffs (see below). A considerable tariff protected the infant industries of the United States throughout the critical stages of industrialization and beyond. Thanks to immigration, rapidly growing fertility, territorial expansion, and its wide-ranging endowment of natural resources, the United States, alone amongst the second wave of industrial powers could shelter behind its tariff walls. For many decades, American manufactures focused on satisfying the domestic market; it was far less dependent on exports than any other significant industrial economy. Also, as demonstrated above, the federal government played a vital role in the emerging American specialization in precision machine tools and interchangeable parts. Establishing and improving patent protections (1790, 1793, and 1836), and creating institutions like the Smithsonian (1846) helped to support invention and to protect innovators. On the other hand, however, the federal government's bumbling efforts to create a national bank unsettled the capital market, slowed development and increased American dependence on Europeans for investment. The U.S. government thus played an essential if not overt role in the American industrial revolution.

MANAGEMENT MATTERED

Despite the immense opportunities provided by the expanding population of the United States, it took more than technological expertise, access to capital, resources and transportation, or government protection to succeed. Even the most profitable manufactures faced ceaseless hazards: the ups and downs of the economy; natural disasters; fire; and labor discontent. The paper mill owners of Berkshire county in Massachusetts enjoyed an incredibly favorable business situation in almost every way, but in the three decades from 1827 to 1857, of the 136 men who founded or took over mills, only 70 (51%) lasted 10 years. Of those 70, 8 failed or suspended payments at least once during that period. An in-depth reconstruction of their account books shows that it was not until 1862 that the mill-owners developed sufficient accounting tools to recognize that they were frequently selling goods below cost.[18] To avoid the uncertainties of the market and the difficulties of maintaining family firms or small partnerships while taking advantage of new managerial techniques, owners increasingly turned to a more professional class of managers. Entrepreneurs and managers collaborated through newly forged business associations and made the most of their access to technically savvy workers. They also brought in partners with commercial expertise. The rise of professional managers, the formation of integrated corporate divisions, and the growing ability to fix wages and prices had, by the closing decades of the nineteenth century, created a more modern corporate economy.[19]

THE COURSE OF AMERICAN INDUSTRIAL GROWTH

Industrialization in the United States was fueled by population growth, dependent on internal improvements in transportation, protected by government action and paid for by the profits of agriculture, both slave and free. The rapidly growing population was the primary market for domestic manufactures. Entrepreneurs took advantage of tariff rates of at least 25%. Throughout the century, tariffs enabled American industry to resist the onslaught of European competition. It is no accident that Francis Cabot Lowell lobbied forcefully to raise the tariff rates from relatively low levels in 1816. The American industrial economy failed to substitute for British goods during the era of the blockade and war (1807–1815). When peace returned, many manufacturers could not compete without the virtual monopoly. The seeds of industrial growth were laid in the 1820s and accelerated in the 1830s with the growth of mechanized textile and shoe/boot industries. It is worth noting that the British industrial revolution was essentially complete by this time.

REGIONAL GROWTH

American industrialization was regional; it was centered in New England and the Middle Atlantic states of New Jersey, Delaware, Pennsylvania, and

New York. As late as 1860, these two areas generated 71% of U.S. manufacturing output. Both the geographical and product base of American industrialization expanded in the 1840s and 1850s as the iron and machine-
building industries (sewing machines, reapers, locomotives, etc.) boomed
while the Midwest began its industrial ascent. It was this era that saw the
United States push beyond Smithian growth to experience an industrial revolution. The motor for this growth was the use of anthracite coal in blast
furnaces to make pig iron. The first such furnace fired in 1840 and by 1853,
there were 121 in operation that made 45% of all American iron. Thus,
the United States, like Great Britain 70 years before, experienced significant
growth in textile manufacturing that preceded widespread industrialization.
Only when other industries like iron and coal joined textiles in the industrial mix did revolutionary conditions emerge. On the eve of the Civil War,
U.S. population reached 31.4 million—significantly less than that of France
(37.4 million)—but greater than that of the United Kingdom (26.6 million). By 1860, the United States was the world's second industrial nation
and was poised for further rapid growth in the second half of the nineteenth
century.[20]

CRYSTAL PALACE

In industrial terms, the American "coming of age" took place at the Crystal
Palace Exhibition of 1851 (see Chapter 4). Although the American exhibit
was quite small, the quality was impressive. Cyrus Hall McCormick's mechanical reaper, Charles Goodyear's India rubber life-raft and Samuel Colt's
six-shot pistol all won prestigious medals and Europeans publicly took notice
of American technology and metal-working skills. Success in the world of
sport even played a role in winning favorable publicity: the yacht *America*
defeated the pride of Great Britain, the *Titania*, in a race that has been per-
petuated as the America's Cup. The *Liverpool Times* fretted, "The Yankees
are no longer to be ridiculed, much less despised. The new world is burst-
ing into greatness—walking past the old world, as the Americans did to the
yachts. . . . America, in her own phrase, is 'going ahead' and will assuredly
pass us unless we accelerate our speed."[21] From humble beginnings, it was
clear that by 1850, the industrial revolution had reached a point that some
U.S. manufactured goods could compete on the world market.

BELGIUM AND THE GERMAN LANDS

BELGIUM, THE GERMAN LANDS, AND THE LEGACY OF FRANCE

Although Belgium (part of the Kingdom of Holland 1815–1830) and
western Germany had manufactured goods for the European and world

market for centuries, their push toward an industrial revolution was jump-started by their incorporation into France. Belgium was an integral part of France for nearly 20 years (1795–1814) and the German-speaking region on the west bank of the Rhine spent almost 15 years as part of Napoleonic France. Both regions experienced rapid industrial growth during French rule. Their skilled workers, ambitious entrepreneurs, and ample assets of quality coal and iron took full advantage of French institutions and access to the vast imperial market. Imperial French control also broke down the backward social and cultural attitudes and regional fragmentation of these regions that had stymied earlier government efforts to erect a well-ordered state that sustained the needs of entrepreneurs. Mechanization, technological modernization, and factory-building occurred in both areas. After the breakup of the Empire, Belgium became part of the Kingdom of Holland, while the most economically advanced sections of German-speaking Europe were given by the victorious Allies—deliberately—to Prussia in hopes of erecting a bulwark against French revival. By ensuring that this region, with its vast industrial potential, became part of a powerful state, the Treaty of Vienna had a powerful impact on the emergence of a united Germany and contributed greatly to the emergence of an industrial revolution in the German lands.

TARIFFS

Like all the first-generation follower industrial nations, Belgium and the major states of western Germany (Prussia, Bavaria, Württemberg, and Hesse-Darmstadt) could not withstand British competition in the cotton textile and metalworking sectors. Although these regions had numerous machine-building workshops, advanced textile technology, and numerous innovative entrepreneurs particularly in the Ruhr and around the Belgian cities of Liège and Verviers, these industries experienced a sharp setback with the breakup of the Napoleonic preferential trade zone covering much of northwestern Europe. Until 1830, Belgium benefited from access to the Netherlands and its colonies, but these markets were no substitute for those of Imperial France. None of the German states wholeheartedly embraced industrialization until the late 1820s. All enacted limitations on the use of machines and the building of factories while most maintained guild-based restrictions on labor and output. Even the famous German customs union, the Zollverein, began slowly in 1818 when Prussia began an attempt to eliminate tolls on goods traveling between the two (separated) halves of the country.

By erecting only moderate tariffs, both the Zollverein and Belgium recognized their dependence on trade for the products of their industries. Without an essential raw material like cotton, neither the German lands nor Belgium had the economic leverage to avoid the potential retaliation of raised tariff rates on their exports. It was, however, only in 1828–1834 that the Zollverein grew to become a free-trade zone that included nearly all of German-speaking Europe other than Austria. Tariffs avoided the wholesale destruction of infant industries that occurred in France and the United States after the end of the Napoleonic wars. In addition, an expanding trading bloc would, in the words of Prussian Finance Minister Friedrich von Motz, promote modernization, "bigger industry" and "superior fabrication."[22] The extension of the Zollverein encouraged standardizing the currency and the building of railroads which multiplied the effects of free trade.

COMPETITION

Both Belgium and the German lands recognized that tariffs were only a temporary solution. Individually, over the course of a decade beginning in the late 1820s, political decision makers recognized what industrial entrepreneurs had realized much earlier—that to be competitive, they would have to adopt British techniques and adapt them to local circumstances while protecting and developing traditional economic strengths. This dawning recognition led the governments of these countries to fashion a very different sort of activist approach to economic development than took place in the United Kingdom, France, or the United States. Some aspects of state involvement were relatively short-term as with the support of railroad building. Others were longer-term in outlook; these measures included the negotiation of commercial treaties and the creation of banks. In Prussia, direct state control of a considerable number of industrial enterprises from textile factories, to iron foundries and chemical plants to flour mills and other important economic institutions like the Overseas Trading Corporation encouraged and permitted an approach to economic policy that contained the germ of centralized planning.

EDUCATION

Education was perhaps the most important of the long-term investments in competitiveness undertaken by the states of German central Europe. Imitating and, in some places, continuing the French educational model, many German states focused on education as a means of competing with the British. Where the French focused on science and mathematics, the Germans stressed practical application, effectively extending technological training to more people than anywhere else. Christian Wilhelm Peter Beuth (1781–1853) who headed the Department of Trade and Industry for 30 critical years (1815–1845) was Prussia's Chaptal. He founded the Berlin Technical Institute and played the key role in creating the influential public-private

Association for the Promotion of Industrial Knowledge in Prussia while overseeing a broadly-based improvement of Prussian technology. The modern research laboratory was born at Giessen in 1825 under the direction of Justus von Liebig (1803–1873) whose "hands on" yet systematic approach to teaching and finding practical solutions to chemical problems became the model for German higher education. German universities also emerged as effective centers of scientific and technological research, tackling industrial problems with academic discipline. In the German lands, as in France, but unlike Great Britain and the United States, a high percentage of physicians, teachers, bureaucrats, and other professionals went to university where they received a strong grounding in scientific and technological issues. Beyond the universities, polytechnical schools mushroomed. By 1850, they enrolled about 5,000 students. These schools morphed into full-scale technical colleges (*technische Hochshulen*), which facilitated the emergence of an influential elite with extensive scientific knowledge and ties both to business and to government. As machinery grew more complex and scientific advance became an increasingly necessary part of improving production, the technological expertise fostered by the technical colleges, research laboratories and universities gave Germany a competitive edge. This became apparent to all when the basis of industrial development shifted at the end of the nineteenth century. German industrial entrepreneurs who directed large enterprises also increasingly needed higher education. In 1851–1870 more than 80% had higher education. Of that total, 38% was academic, 15% attended a business or technical school, and the rest had a more practical education.[23] In the twentieth century, the German educational system became the model for the industrialized world.

PERSONAL TECHNOLOGY TRANSFER

Much of the technology transfer into Belgium (both before and after independence) was accomplished by individuals. British technicians and mechanics emigrated to set up their own establishments and to take advantage of the opportunities afforded by their specialized or craft knowledge. An English mechanic named William Cockerill (1759–1832) emigrated to Verviers in French-held Belgium in 1798 to build five mechanized mills to spin wool, beginning a rapid modernization of the moribund woolens industry in that region. The first firm to innovate remained the largest single producer for the rest of the nineteenth century. Flush with this success, Cockerill, his three sons William Jr., John and James, along with his son-in-law, James Hodson established a workshop in 1805 to build machines in Liège. The demand for textile machines spawned a host of orders and the quality of Cockerill construction guaranteed sales. A supplemental workshop was established in Paris to supply the French market and Cockerill spinning machines also equipped the woolen industries of Prussia and Saxony. In the hot-house atmosphere of the Continental System, the Cockerill establishment swiftly became a vertically integrated enterprise comprising coal and later iron mining, iron smelting, pig-iron processing, metal fabrication, and machine-building.

After 1815, the Cockerills introduced puddling and the blast-furnace to the continent and built the first locomotives and iron steamships outside of Britain: all with the direct financial support of King William I of the Netherlands. In engineering and metallurgy, the Cockerill enterprises now centered at Seraing (a mansion bought from the King for a pittance) were among the largest and most productive in the world. At their height, the machine-building shops alone employed 2,700 workers and helped to naturalize high-pressure steam-engine construction in the region. The weaving of woolens was mechanized after 1814, again with machines built by the Cockerills. John moved to Berlin where he set up a wool-spinning factory, established a satellite machine-building shop and bought and refurbished three other woolen spinning mills. William Jr. remained in Berlin. James built a machine-building workshop in Aachen. A contemporary, Désiré Nisard of France, remarked of Cockerill, "His establishment in Seraing is the largest in Europe . . . he is indeed the new prince-sovereign of Seraing with lieutenants all over the world."[24] This spurt of metallurgical development spurred complementary growth in several districts in Belgium and western Germany as local entrepreneurs often paired with English engineers or technicians rushed to open coal mines, modern blast furnaces, puddling plants, and machine-shops in hopes of exploiting the same deep vein of demand tapped by the Cockerills.

These two generations of entrepreneurs also demonstrated the limits of personal involvement in managing a far-flung and diverse enterprise. Unlike the Krupp family (see insert), despite all their successes, the Cockerills failed to establish a business structure capable of weathering recessions and the waning of their technological advantages. By the late 1840s, the industrial empire built by the Cockerills had largely passed into the hands of others, demonstrating the growing importance of business organization to long-term industrial success by a family firm.

BANKS

Two banks, the Société Générale de Belgique and the Banque de Belgique, founded in 1822 and 1835 respectively, played major roles in industrialization. These institutions combined commercial banking and long-term investment. Because heavy industry and deep mining were at the heart of Belgian industrialization, the long-term capital needs of new firms were enormous. Even when firms started small, the demands of mechanization and modernization forced them to attract outside funds. Because of the ebb and flow of the economy, eventually the banks came to control many enterprises. This situation lasted for many decades and the "managerial capitalism" practiced by the directors of these banks laid the foundations of the industrial revolution in Belgium. In Prussia, financial institutions, notably the Darmstadt Bank, the Discount Bank, and the Berlin Commercial Company, also fostered industrialization by helping to sidestep a generalized and long-standing shortage of investment capital. In 1856, the French consul in Leipzig remarked that "as much energy is being put into covering Germany with a network of credit-banks as has been put into creating a railway network."[25]

RAILROADS

In German central Europe, as in North America, the construction of a network of railroads transformed the economy. Not only did investment in agriculture decline at the expense of industry, but railroad-building also necessitated the development of heavy industry which became an essential element of industrialization. Railroad construction accelerated economic development throughout the German lands as mines, forges, and workshops modernized and adapted to meet rapidly growing demand. Belgium may have boasted the first railroad line in continental Europe stretching from Brussels to Malines and completed in May 1835, but it was closely followed by various German states notably Prussia and Saxony. The Saxon state strongly supported the group of entrepreneurs seeking to construct a line to link Leipzig and Dresden. The joint-stock company formed in 1835 received powerful encouragements in the form of a guarantee of a 3.5% return to investors and a pledge to buy shares if problems of capitalization occurred. The route opened in stages in 1837–1838 to be the first major line on the continent. In the late 1830s, partly for military and partly for economic reasons, both Prussia and Austria became enthusiastic railroad builders. As a result, by 1850, the German lands boasted 3,761 miles of track, nearly double that of France. For the next two decades, railroads absorbed 60–70% of the capital invested in the entire industrial sector, so that by unification, Germany boasted 10,768 miles of track.[26]

INDUSTRIALIZATION IN PRUSSIA

Railroad fever and a burgeoning population spurred the growth of Prussia. As in Belgium, heavy demand for iron and coal stimulated modernization, technological improvement, and expansion. At the same time, factories blossomed as entrepreneurs took advantage of widening market access, the low cost of labor, and falling transport costs. By 1850, about one-third of the nonfarm working population of Prussia toiled in a factory. As part of this trend, steam engines cropped up everywhere. The number of steam engines grew from a mere 419 in 1837 to 1,444 12 years later. Saxony,

The House of Krupp

The Krupp metalworking dynasty dates from 1587 in Essen, in the Ruhr region on the west bank of the Rhine River in Germany. This family made and lost several fortunes, but the rise of Alfred Krupp (1812–1887) to worldwide prominence as the "Cannon King" of the Franco-Prussian War (1870–1871) sheds light on the nature of entrepreneurship during the industrial revolution. His father had squandered the family fortune leaving only considerable debts and a small water-powered steel foundry. Alfred had to leave school at the age of 14 to take over the foundering enterprise.

After eight lean years, Krupp took immediate advantage of the Zollverein. In 1834, he embarked on a sales trip to southern Germany where he solicited more orders than the tiny foundry with its nine employees could deliver. After borrowing money from a cousin, these orders enabled him to purchase a steam engine and expand the workforce. Raising his sights higher, Krupp engaged in industrial espionage. He spent 15 months in England under an assumed name. By imitating a gentleman, he gained access to foundries and rolling mills. His early experience and English sojourn taught Krupp that the best route to consistent profits was to make finished products of the best quality, which was easy to do with the high grade iron and coal of the Ruhr. The "secret" of English success was "how huge a market can be conquered by a good product."

Upon his return, a short recession of 1839 endangered the business. Krupp had to take on an additional partner and get credit from a local bank. He used the funds to build a modern smelting plant with a huge workshop attached. Another correction in 1845–1849 enabled Krupp to buy out his brothers and take over sole control. This buyout took place as he benefited from his brother Fritz's technical expertise. Fritz invented a machine constructed of steel that made 150 spoons or forks a day. It inaugurated a new phase in the mass production of tableware and earned the House of Krupp enormous profits long after its inventor had been squeezed out.

After the Revolution of 1848, orders poured in. Krupp made his fortune by expanding from steel tableware and other sundry items into railroad and steamboat supply. The sale of cast-steel locomotive wheels, rails and fittings convinced a Jewish banker, Salomon Oppenheim of Cologne, to lend Krupp enough money on easy terms for Krupp to expand rapidly. His workforce grew from 76 in 1847 to 1,000 a decade later. Krupp advertised his firm's technical prowess and fine workmanship with eye-catching displays at the Crystal Palace Exhibition of 1851 and the Paris Universal Exposition of 1855. Although Krupp tried to make and sell arms in the early 1840s, he did not make his first sale until the late 1850s. The Prussian state only began to order cast-steel cannon from him in 1859. Rapidly, the advantages of these weapons became clear and Krupp sold to the governments of Egypt, Switzerland, Spain, Netherlands, Austria, and even the United Kingdom. The success of his weapons in the Franco-Prussian War earned Krupp the "Cannon King" moniker, although his detractors called him the "Merchant of Death."

Luck and riding the tide of the booming economy made Alfred and his heirs rich and famous. Krupp remained a major arms manufacturer through the Nazi period. Despite going public, the firm remained in family hands until 1968, more than 400 years after the family first began its metallurgical career.

the traditional industrial center of the German lands, had only 197 steam engines in 1846. This comparison demonstrates the modern, mechanized character of Prussian factory production and the seeds of later even more rapid growth.

SMITHIAN GROWTH IN THE GERMAN LANDS

With the population of the German lands rising from 25 million in 1815 to 35.5 million in 1850 to outstrip France and then to 41 million in 1870, demand boomed and the labor supply increased impressively, despite the emigration of more than 2.5 million people in that period. Urbanization grew even more rapidly. As a result of these conditions, the use of child, female, and unfree labor was far less and shorter on the continent of Europe than in Britain or the United States. The consumption of raw cotton increased nearly sixfold 1820–1850 while the much larger woolen sector grew by a third. Coal production tripled and iron output grew by a factor of 11.5 to reach 529,000 tons.

VIOLENCE

As always, the rapid transformation of the industrial economy left home-bound workers in domestic industries behind. A major outbreak of machine-breaking occurred in 1844 as 5,000 handloom weavers in Silesia attempted to destroy the factories and mansions of innovative entrepreneurs. Riots and strikes in many other rapidly industrializing areas broke out in sympathy. As in France, this violence took place during the initial stages of industrialization and presaged the outbreak of revolution (in 1848). The speed of development in the German lands meant that, like the Luddites, the Silesian machine-breakers were the last gasp of practitioners of an outdated mode of production. The foundations of growth were so well-established that although the Revolution of 1848 and the wars with Denmark and Austria slowed down the economy, these events did not sidetrack the rapid transition from Smithian growth in the 1830s and 1840s to an industrial revolution in the 1850s and 1860s.[27]

PRUSSIA AND GERMANY

As in the United States and Belgium, one of the most striking characteristics of the industrialization of the German lands was its speed. Although the pace of Smithian growth accelerated in the 1830s and 1840s, once railroad construction began in earnest, industrial transformation truly took off. This growth was centered in the expanding state of Prussia. Prussia mined almost all of Germany's zinc, 90% of the coal, 77% of the lead, and 66% of the iron ore. At the same time, Prussia produced 90% of the pig iron and nearly all of the steel. Almost 80% of the flax spindles, two-thirds of the steam engines and over half of the machinery to work wool were located on Prussian soil. Among the major industries of Germany, only the cotton sector escaped Prussian domination.[28]

GERMAN RATES OF GROWTH

Overall, the German lands experienced impressive industrial growth in the two decades before unification in 1871. Textiles remained the largest sector, employing over three-quarters of a million men, women and children with woolens leading the way both in output and in employment. Despite rapid growth, at unification, the German cotton industry was only one-sixth the size of Britain's. Coal production flourished. In a mere 11 years (1860–1871), production grew from 16.7 to 37.9 million tons. Germany emerged as the second largest coal producer in the world, far behind the United Kingdom, but considerably ahead of the United States, France, and Belgium. In percentage terms, the growth of iron mining was even more impressive. In 1850, German output was only one-sixth that of the United Kingdom and less than half that of France. Two decades later, Germany mined 4.3 million tons of iron ore, almost five times as much as in 1850. Pig iron production more than kept pace, growing from a mere 130,000 tons in 1834 to a million tons in 1870. A more indicative sign of the transformation taking place was that real national product per capita expanded 2.0–2.5% annually in the 1840s, at 2.5% in the 1850s, and up to 3.0% in the 1860s. Industrial production grew at a blistering 4.8% annual pace in 1850–1873 while total national income increased by a quarter, faster than either Britain or France during their phases of rapid growth, but approximately the same as American growth during the same period. Real per capita income expanded 0.8% annually and money wages increased about 25% between 1820 and 1850 and a spectacular additional 50% in the succeeding two decades. The industrial revolution in Germany was fast and furious.[29]

THE INDUSTRIAL REVOLUTION IN BELGIUM—A REGIONAL DEVELOPMENT

By political accident, Belgium was the second industrial nation. Had this relatively compact region with a population of about 3 million in 1800 and 4.3 million in 1850, remained part of France or the Netherlands, its impressive growth would have been subsumed in larger patterns of economic performance. The inclusion of so little agricultural land within its political boundaries and the newness of its political culture facilitated government policies that firmly focused on industrial development. Belgium systematically attracted British engineers and technologists as a means of technological modernization. Coal production boomed, growing from an annual output of 2.4 million metric tons in 1830 to an impressive 10.2 million in 1860. Pig iron production increased nearly fourfold from 95,000 to 366,000 metric tons in the same period. As impressive as these achievements are, it was only its truncated national boundaries that made Belgian industrial development comparable to Britain's.[30]

By adopting and adapting the elements of British industrialization suitable for continental conditions, in the decades after 1815, Belgium was able to use heavy industry, mining, and engineering complemented by the woolen and cotton textile sectors to forge its industrial revolution, reversing the proportions of the British model. The transformation of the economy occurred at a rapid pace. Export-driven like its European competitors, Belgium exported not only finished products and natural resources, but also technology (both British and its own), entrepreneurs, engineers, skilled workers, and capital to make itself indispensable to its larger neighbors. Belgium took advantage of its position as a close follower of the British to create a shadow path to industrial society. The Belgian industrial revolution was basically complete by 1860, a generation after the United Kingdom's.[31]

THE TIMING OF INDUSTRIAL REVOLUTIONS

This survey of other paths to an industrial revolution clarifies the time lag between the emergence of the British version of industrialization and those of the closest follower nations. Britain began its revolutionary transformation in the late eighteenth century and a fully realized industrial society was in place by 1850. Belgium started in the 1830s and finished in 1860. After fits and starts, France began its revolution in the 1820s, but, like Britain, it took nearly 50 years to complete. Of the initial group of followers, the United States and the German lands experienced the most rapid and most thorough industrial transformations. In the United States, the critical decades were the 1840s and 1850s, while in German central Europe the vital developments took place in the 1850s and 1860s. The duration of the British industrial revolution stemmed from the difficulties associated with innovation. For France, the process of industrialization seemed interminable for fundamentally political reasons. In Belgium, the United States and the German lands, the industrial revolution was more rapid and based on different needs and requirements. These nations also benefited from not having to develop the technological expertise, methods of production, or capital needed to industrialize. The ability to borrow these essential aspects of industrialization goes a long way toward explaining the rapidity of industrialization in these follower nations. Twenty years may sound like a long time to a present-day observer, but in the nineteenth century, the pace of change associated with an industrial revolution was dizzying.

This comparative survey of paths to industrialization also demonstrates the distinct challenges faced by entrepreneurs, government officials, and workers in different times and places. Although there were sharp, short economic depressions after 1815, until 1873, these slumps did not have the same sort of devastating economic consequences that characterized earlier downturns. As a result, the paths to industrial society of Great Britain and France were far rockier than the more direct, fortuitous routes taken by the next generation of industrial nations. These historical examples demonstrate that economic models must match up with general economic realities if the goal is to spark an industrial revolution. The variations on the role of the state, trade, and empire, the place of the textile sector, the function of metallurgy and mining, the means of acquiring technology, and the involvement of the working classes discussed here also show that even the most verdant industrial pathways must be pruned, fertilized and tended if they are to bear fruit.

7

INDUSTRIALIZATION AND THE NEW WORLD ORDER

The industrial revolution was both the cause and the effect of the domination of the world by Europeans. If earlier economic developments (see Chapter 2) had facilitated the emergence of a world economy driven by European needs and demands, in the nineteenth century, the power differential between the "West and the rest" became much more pronounced. Europeans and their descendants living in North America, South Africa, Australia, New Zealand, Algeria, and many other places scattered around the world became the masters of the planet. The industrial revolution facilitated the development of Western military superiority and the new, improved means of transportation tied the globe together in a far more concrete manner allowing the exploitation of vast new areas. At minimal cost, Europeans and their descendants came to enjoy an unprecedented degree of world domination as a result of the industrial revolution.

IMPERIALISM

THE DOMINATION OF THE WEST

Western domination was expressed in a number of subtle and not-so-subtle fashions. One of the most remarkable factors concerns population. We have traced the growth of European population. Just as striking, however, is the shift in Europe's share of the world population; it reached its all-time historical peak of 24% around 1900. In 1650, that proportion had been only a little over 18%, in 1750 a shade over 19%, in 1850 almost 23%. (In 2000, that figure had fallen to less than 12%!)[1]

LABOR FLOWS—VOLUNTARY

One reason for the spike in European population was heavy emigration. That emigration reached impressive proportions before the industrial revolution, but during and after industrialization, it grew even greater. Sixty million people left Europe amidst rapid industrial development in the century 1840–1940. Eight million left between 1850 and 1880. This emigration was overwhelmingly (85%) from Great Britain and Germany and went mostly to North America and South America. The United States, Argentina, Canada, and Brazil absorbed the most emigrants, in that order.

LABOR FLOWS—INVOLUNTARY

It is also worth noting that involuntary emigration from Africa to the Americas continued as the slave trade remained in operation to feed the remaining Spanish colonies and Brazil. By the time slavery was outlawed in these places near the end of the nineteenth century, between two and three million more slaves had been brought to the New World. In addition, more than 550,000 inhabitants of the subcontinent of India migrated to the British, French, and Dutch islands of the Caribbean as contract laborers. Nearly a million more went to British and French colonies in the Indian Ocean. Over 300,000 Chinese workers also emigrated to British colonies in the Pacific Ocean. This labor was essential to the building of transportation and communication links that permitted the exploitation of the agricultural and mineral wealth of both the New World and the European colonial empires. All these groups of immigrants also contributed to the stock of entrepreneurship that was essential to the economic development of all these areas. Without the migration of Africans, Indians, and Chinese into colonial and developing societies, Europeans and their descendants could not have exploited the economic opportunities they found throughout the world.

TRADE EMPIRE

Trade endured as a potent weapon in the hands of Europeans. Throughout the nineteenth century, Europeans and their descendants—including the United States—built powerful industrial complexes behind high tariff walls to protect them from competition. Once those industrial machines were humming, then the powers of Europe used their military might (based on superior technology) to force other areas of the world to give them access to their lands and markets on favorable terms. This process included the Russian expansion into Asia and the United States' push toward the Pacific as well as the rapid growth of European overseas empires.

Europeans and their descendants wanted three things: natural resources, access to additional consumers, and to prevent competition. "Free trade" was an implement of economic warfare that allowed more advanced economies to dominate others.

Friedrich List (1789–1846)

A man of many careers—economist, professor, journalist, politician, and business-man—List is best known for his attacks on Adam Smith's conception of the benefits of free trade and for helping to bring about the Prussian customs union, the Zollverein. Although he admired many aspects of British society and culture, List recognized that stronger economies could prevent the emergence of competition through free trade. Following a historical resume of how others had dealt with the issues of protection and development, in the *National System of Political Economy* (1841), he described how Britain sought to take advantage of free trade in Germany after the Napoleonic Wars to prevent competition.

> More and more the opinion spread at the time that the English Government were favour-ing in an unprecedented manner a scheme for glutting the markets on the Continent with manufactured goods in order to stifle the Continental manufactures in the cradle. This idea has been ridiculed, but it was natural enough that it should prevail, first, because this glutting really took place in such a manner as though it had been deliberately planned; and, secondly, because a celebrated member of Parliament, Mr Henry Brougham (after-wards Lord Brougham), had openly said, in 1815, "that it was well worth while to incur a loss on the exportation of English manufactures in order to stifle in the cradle the foreign manufactures."(*) This idea of this lord, since so renowned as a philanthropist, cosmopolist, and Liberal, was repeated ten years later almost in the same words by Mr. Hume, a member of Parliament not less distinguished for liberalism, when he ex-pressed a wish that "Continental manufactures might be nipped in the bud." At length the prayer of the Prussian manufacturers found a hearing . . . The Prussian customs tariff of 1818 answered, for the time in which it was established, all the requirements of Prussian industry, without in any way overdoing the principle of protection or unduly interfering with the country's beneficial intercourse with foreign countries.

*Report of the Committee of Commerce and Manufactures to the House of Representatives of the Congress of the United States, February 13, 1816.

Source: Friedrich List, *The National System of Political Economy*, trans. Sampson S. Lloyd (1885 [1841]), Book I, Chapter 7.

The symbol of European success at building up their economies was the era of relatively free trade that occurred between 1860 and 1879. Only when the Europeans believed that they required *exclusive* access to markets and materials did the trade barriers go back up and the direct acquisition of colonies accelerate. By 1914, the Western powers ruled 84% of the world's land masses.

THE EXPANSION OF TRADE

Despite these political barriers, transportation links spread, trade boomed, and empires blossomed. From 1850 to 1914, world trade increased almost sixfold, from 15 to 100 billion dollars. Between 1800 and 1913, foreign trade increased from 3% of world output to a whopping 33%.[2] Although most of this expansion was within Europe, intercontinental trade also blossomed. Two-thirds of global imports went to Europe. These imports were composed largely of foodstuffs, including coffee, tea, and sugar, industrial raw materials like cotton, wool, rubber, jute, and silk, and minerals including gold, silver, diamonds, tin, and lead. Half of all exports came from Europe. Overwhelmingly, these exports were the products of industry such as textiles and capital goods such as machinery or construction and building materials. The discrepancy between imports and exports demonstrates the structural trade deficit experienced by many advanced industrial countries that was filled through so-called "invisible exports." Invisible exports included services like shipping and insurance as well as the profits from foreign investment (see below). The industrial revolution made Europe more dependent on the globalization of the economy than ever.[3]

THE EVOLUTION OF EMPIRE

At the height of the industrial revolution, the European nations did not seem as eager to acquire territory as they had been from the sixteenth through eighteenth centuries. In fact, the period after the United States achieved independence in 1783 and following the revolt of most of Spain's colonies (1810–1825), has been described as one of decolonization. This is a mistake. The relationship of Europe and its descendants with the rest of the world was just as rapacious during the century from 1770 to 1870 as it was before or after. The only real differences were the forms that domination took.

The two chief patterns of the evolution of empire during the age of the industrial revolution were the expansion of existing colonies, bases, or possessions into new areas and the further development of what could be termed "economic empire." In Africa, under British and French pressure from north, south and east, small handholds along the sea in Gold Coast (Ghana), Nigeria, Algeria, and South Africa expanded greatly into large, economically important colonies. In Asia, the British continued to acquire territory in the subcontinent of India, and pushed into Malaysia while founding Singapore, but it was the Russian expansion to the Pacific that was the most remarkable imperial accomplishment of the period. In the Americas, the British in Canada, the United States, and the Brazilians also took possession of their interiors. The rest of coastal Africa, the former Spanish colonies of the New World and even China and southeast Asia were not forgotten: European and American business interests acquired control or developed the resources of these areas tying them ever more tightly into the world economy. In the age of the "New Imperialism" from 1870 to 1914, this informal, economic control was frequently transformed into formal political rule.

INDIA

THE JEWEL IN THE CROWN

In the nineteenth century, the subcontinent of India was the most valuable colony in the world. Since the seventeenth century, British influence had been exercised mostly by the East India Company which operated on a charter from the crown. After a mutiny by native elements of the Indian Army in 1857–1858, the British government took direct control of this lucrative region. No matter which British institution controlled the region, native interests took a backseat to those of the conquerors. British power in the subcontinent was the result of many factors, but the exploitation of India enabled and maintained industrialization in the United Kingdom.

In the nineteenth century, India emerged as the linchpin of the British empire and thus of the British economy. The British developed myriad ways to profit from their dominance of the subcontinent. India became a key market for British manufactured goods. In 1854, India absorbed 13% of British trade, behind only the United States. By 1900, the volume of British trade with India had tripled: India now received nearly one-fifth of Britain's imports and exports. British exports to India were almost exclusively cotton textiles and the products of the iron and metallurgical industries. This protected market helped keep these key sectors profitable as their international competitiveness waned.[4]

To prevent competition with Lancashire, the British intentionally deindustrialized India beginning in the late eighteenth century. This was done by manipulations of the tariff and the excise, choking off credit, increasing land prices or rents, and raising transportation prices on goods that were not approved of by the authorities. As India's own industries were throttled by British tariffs and taxes, India became an enormous importer of British textiles. That trade reached 1 million meters in 1814, 13 million in 1820, and by 1890, India imported 2 billion meters of British textiles. To put these numbers into context, where India purchased only one-half of 1% of British cotton goods in 1815, by the eve of World War I, the subcontinent regularly absorbed 40–45% of the output of Lancashire. This vast trade, protected by tariff walls and other measures ensured the continuing profitability of British mills and forced the poor peasants of India to find other means of paying their taxes and making a living.[5]

Having removed one source of livelihood, the British in India, seconded by Indian entrepreneurs, encouraged and/or forced the peasants to cultivate products needed either by Britain or by Britain's other main trading partner in Asia—China. Pushed by the need for revenue, Indians began to generate considerable surpluses of wheat, cotton, jute, and tea that helped to fuel the industrial revolution and the people of Britain. These agricultural exports helped to counterbalance the flood of food and industrial raw materials that entered Britain from outside the Empire.[6]

OPIUM

In a far more insidious decision, British leaders in India provided generous incentives and utilized strong-arm tactics to boost the cultivation of poppy to make opium. Although the opium trade was illegal, British officials encouraged its cultivation and winked at the illegalities. Opium was needed for trade with China: the British were enraged that the Chinese wanted none of their textiles and would only sell their tea, silks, porcelains, and other goods for gold and silver. The evil geniuses of British mercantilism who ran the East India Company devised this alternative strategy—push opium on the Chinese.[7] When the Chinese government attempted to stop the traffic in this drug, the United Kingdom fought wars in 1839–1842 and 1856–1860 to maintain access to the addictions—and pocketbooks—of the people of China. Conducted beneath the barrels of British naval cannon, exports to China quadrupled in 18 years (1850–1868).[8] Chocolate from West Africa, sugar and tobacco from the West Indies, coffee from East Africa and Ceylon, tea from India and Ceylon were addictive, but accepted parts of the human diet. Opium, however, was banned in Britain. Through their Empire, centered in India, the British became the greatest drug pushers the world had ever seen.

THE MILITARY

Trade was only part of the benefits Britain derived from control of India. As India was the linchpin of the British trade structure, so too, India was the anchor of British defense. Britain maintained a huge army in India—this force represented two-thirds of all the men Britain had under arms—paid for by Indian taxpayers without any recourse to Parliament. These regiments could be and were used to fight Britain's wars all over the globe. From the river valleys of China to the plains of Africa to Flanders' fields in the Great War, the British Indian Army fought for the United Kingdom. Despite the vast revenue enjoyed by the British state as landowner to millions of Indian tenants, not to mention collecting traditional sources of income, military expenditures constituted 40% of total Indian revenue in 1885 and when crises occurred, that figure could rise to over 50%. British taxpayers stayed home and enjoyed the benefits of "laissez-faire."[9]

DEVELOPMENT

To exploit this vast area, it first needed to be tied together through transportation and communications links. The first telegraph lines were laid in 1851 on a grid designed by the Governor-General. Military needs consistently trumped commercial considerations—the same was true for the improvements in postal service. The railroad system was the most impressive accomplishment of the British in India. Begun in 1852, by the end of the

Lin Tse-Hsu (1785–1850)
"Letter of Advice to Queen Victoria" (1839)

As Imperial Commissioner in Canton, Lin Tse-Hsu attempted to crack down on the burgeoning opium trade sponsored by the British East India Company. Opium addiction had become a major social problem and the Emperor's son had recently died of an overdose. It was in light of this event that he wrote the letter excerpted below to the Queen of England. His attempts to negotiate an end to opium imports were ignored by the British. Lin Tse-Hsu then seized the vast stores of British goods at Canton, the chief trading port. Britain declared war to protect the opium dealers and the merchants who helped them. The British fleet's technological superiority ensured an easy victory and, in 1842, the treaty ending the conflict legalized the opium trade.

We find your country is sixty or seventy thousand *li* [three *li* make one mile, ordinarily] from China. Yet there are barbarian ships that strive to come here for trade for the purpose of making a great profit. The wealth of China is used to profit the barbarians. That is to say, the great profit made by barbarians is all taken from the rightful share of China. By what right do they then in return use the poisonous drug to injure the Chinese people? Even though the barbarians may not necessarily intend to do us harm, yet in coveting profit to an extreme, they have no regard for injuring others. Let us ask, where is your conscience? I have heard that the smoking of opium is very strictly forbidden by your country; that is because the harm caused by opium is clearly understood. Since it is not permitted to do harm to your own country, then even less should you let it be passed on to the harm of other countries—how much less to China!

We have further learned that in London, the capital of your honorable rule, and in Scotland, Ireland, and other places, originally no opium has been produced. Only in several places of India under your control . . . has opium been planted from hill to hill, and ponds have been opened for its manufacture. For months and years work is continued in order to accumulate the poison. The obnoxious odor ascends, irritating heaven and frightening the spirits. Indeed you, O King, can eradicate the opium plant in these places, hoe over the fields entirely, and sow in its stead the five grains [millet, barley, wheat, etc.]. Anyone who dares again attempt to plant and manufacture opium should be severely punished. This will really be a great, benevolent government policy that will increase the common weal and get rid of evil.

Source: Ssu-yu Teng and John Fairbank, *China's Response to the West* (Cambridge, MA: Harvard University Press, 1954), reprinted in Mark A. Kishlansky, ed., *Sources of World History*, Vol. II (New York: HarperCollins, 1995), 266–69.

decade, India had 432 miles of track. By 1869, the system had grown to 5,000 miles of line and reached an impressive 25,000 by the end of the century. This was more than all the rest of Asia combined; only Russia, the United States, and Canada had more extensive networks. Although the need to move troops from one end of the country to the other was a major issue in determining which lines received concessions, the railroad system tied India together much more concretely than ever before.[10]

AND ITS COST

Britain borrowed huge sums to pay for the railroads, telegraph lines, and postal network. These sums were to be repaid by Indian taxpayers. But, yet again, the British stacked the deck to maintain maximum profit for themselves and heighten the burden on the people of India. As British lobbyist Hyde Clark put it, "the real operation, after all, is to make the Hindoos [Hindus of India] form the railways, and enable us to reap a large portion of the profits."[11] When the United Kingdom went on the gold standard in 1821, Indian currency, the rupee, remained based on silver. As British control of the subcontinent grew, so too did British control over the currency. In 1874, to offset rapidly growing Indian exports to Britain, the United Kingdom devalued the rupee a whopping 80% against the pound sterling. This measure kept British goods competitive in India. But the devaluation also meant that in just two decades (1874–1894), India had to pay 50% more money to service its debt. Britain bled India dry.[12]

A WORLD ECONOMY

SPECIALIZATION IN A WORLD ECONOMY

The relationship between India and the United Kingdom demonstrates the evolving European specialization within the world economy. As the power differential between metropoles and colonies widened, imperialist nations appropriated all manufacturing activity and forced their colonies to produce and to consume as they wanted and needed. Europe became ever more industrialized, ever more urban, while the rest of the world deindustrialized and/or focused on providing raw materials and markets to feed the hungry maw of Europe's mechanized factories and teeming masses.

No longer did Europe produce nearly all its own food or most of the raw materials its industries needed. The United Kingdom and the German lands had produced high-quality woolens since the Middle Ages. By the end of the nineteenth century, however, both countries were dependent on the Southern Hemisphere for raw wool. The farmers of Europe that could not specialize in a high-value product like meat, milk, cheese, wine, or olive oil suffered, but the economic reality of the global economy meant that it was significantly cheaper to allow areas thousands of miles away—Australia, New Zealand, Argentina, and South Africa—to supply almost three-quarters of the world's wool rather than to mobilize the land and labor needed to produce it domestically.[13]

Only the rapid expansion of trade could enable this shift in the world economy. It should not surprise that the most thoroughly industrialized areas were the ones where trade was most developed. For Britain, per capita trade came to £17, 7 shillings in 1870. Only Belgium was comparable. For France it was £6, 4 shillings, for Germany £5, 6 shillings, and for the United States

£4, 9 shillings. International trade—which had increased from $700 million in 1750 to $38,170 million in 1913—was the lubrication that facilitated Europe's unprecedented domination of the world economy.[14]

CAPITAL INVESTED

European specialization within the world economy was first enabled and then maintained by the advantages in economic organization that stemmed from the industrial revolution. The unheard of profits generated by industrialization widened the gap between the West and the rest. British capital was essential to the industrial revolutions of the United States and the German lands. At the very least, British investments speeded up the timing and pace of industrialization in those areas. French and Belgian capital played important roles in central and eastern Europe. The British were the first to shift their investment strategy away from Europe and North America toward the "undeveloped" world. In the 1860s, more than half of British capital invested abroad (more than £250 million) was in Europe and the United States, but, on the eve of World War I, that percentage had fallen to a quarter. Between 1855 and 1870, the United Kingdom annually invested £29 million abroad. By 1873, the United Kingdom's investments overseas were nearing the billion pound mark. Nor were the British alone. By 1870, Germany and France had each invested almost half a billion pounds abroad, which represented a twenty-five-fold increase since 1820.[15]

Territorial control by a European power could protect these investments and help them to pay. Thanks to its industrial domination, the United Kingdom had the most accumulated profits to invest. Some of this capital enabled the follower nations to develop, but much of it was invested abroad. The British Empire and informal empire in Latin America provided the opportunities for extreme profits that their mature domestic market no longer created. In the continent of Africa, the opportunities for "superprofits" available in the late nineteenth century included the diamond and gold mines of South Africa, shares in the company that built and maintained the Suez Canal linking the Mediterranean and the Red Sea and the loans to the spendthrift governments of North Africa.[16] These investments were an important reason why the United Kingdom extended its Empire into Egypt and from there a thousand miles south along the Nile River. They extended their control the same distance north of their original colony at Capetown in South Africa.

THE GOLD STANDARD

Investments abroad were facilitated in numerous ways. Monetary stability was increasingly ensured as European central banks took over the issuing of money and built up reserves of precious metals to cushion inflationary pressures. The United Kingdom took the lead once again by creating a "gold standard" in 1821 to support the pound. At the same time that the European nations moved toward establishing "free trade" in the 1860s, they also adopted the gold standard for their currencies making them fully convertible. By 1874, the gold standard was in place among the industrialized nations—except in the United States which also used silver to back the dollar—and a multilateral system of world trading pivoting on the financial institutions of the City of London emerged. As the hinge of world finance, the United Kingdom derived enormous profits from insurance, brokerage, and commissions throughout the second half of the nineteenth century and beyond.[17]

SHIPPING

The final component of industrial advantage was in shipping. The continuing technological improvement of sailing ships helped Europeans and their descendants dominate the global shipping trade. When steam and iron ships became important aspects of the carrying trade in the 1860s, the technological and industrial requirements of building and maintaining a merchant fleet increased exponentially. As in so many other domains, the United Kingdom was the primary beneficiary, although the United States, Germany, and the Netherlands also had or acquired significant merchant marines. As world shipping tonnage increased from 4 million net tons in 1800 to 9 million in 1850 and 20 million in 1880, the British retained a consistent one-third to one-half of the fleet. Until the 1870s, the earnings from shipping were greater than that from overseas interest and dividends. Thus, during the age of imperialism, the four pillars of European, but especially of British profits, were (1) trade profits primarily from the sale of manufactured goods; (2) services including the return on investments; (3) insurance, brokerage, and commissions; and (4) shipping. As the industrial economies matured and their standard of living improved, many countries saw the profits of the third and fourth categories compensate for growing trade deficits. Such a situation was possible only because of the enormous differential in power between the West and the rest.[18]

TECHNOLOGY AND EMPIRE

The territorial expansion of Europeans and their descendants was the result of important technological developments. As discussed above, railroads were essential to the exploitation of vast stretches of the globe. The steamboat was transformed into a flat-bottomed weapon of war by the British Royal Navy in 1823. River steamers played a major role in extending British power up the waterways of southeast Asia and Africa. As steam engines and then in the 1860s ironclad ships and high explosive shells became the dominant technological advantages, soon only countries with major metallurgical and chemical establishments could build a modern navy.

Continuous improvements to firearms allowed small numbers of trained Western troops to defeat huge numbers of less well-armed native opponents.

This display at an industrial exposition, located next to sewing machines and harvesting machines, demonstrates the unbeatable weaponry easily available to the Western powers but impossible to make without an industrialized economy. The Burndy Library, Cambridge, Massachusetts

Percussion caps—invented by a Scottish clergyman named Alexander Forsyth in 1807—permitted a musket to fire in almost any weather. In the 1860s, breech-loading rather than muzzle-loading weapons became practical infantry weapons thanks to improvements in machine tools and metallurgy.

More accurate and with a much greater range, breech-loading rifles were an almost unbeatable advantage that was accentuated in the 1860s with the invention of the repeating rifle that could fire six times a minute. Thanks to a host of such improvements, by the 1890s, a European infantryman lying down under cover could fire fifteen rounds in 15 seconds accurately at targets up to a half mile distant, no matter the weather. The patenting of a rapid-fire machine gun in 1884 widened the technological advantage to unimaginable proportions.

MALARIA

Among the key technological breakthroughs that enabled the expansion of European empire was a prophylactic for malaria. This disease decimated people of European descent who entered the interior of Africa. Malaria (from the Italian *mal'aria* or bad air) has probably killed more humans than any other disease. It was not until 1880 that a French scientist, Alphonse

Laveran, isolated the cause of the disease and only in 1897 was the vector, the *Anopheles* mosquito identified. As early as the seventeenth century, Jesuit priests found a treatment—the bark of the cinchona tree. The difficulty of acquiring enough bark, which grew only in limited areas of the Andes Mountains of South America, made the treatment of limited utility. In 1820, two French chemists, Pierre Joseph Peletier and Joseph Bienaimé Caventou, extracted an alkaloid from cinchona bark—quinine. By 1830, the drug was being manufactured in sufficient quantity for general use and began being tested. Once dosages had been standardized—it worked best if the bloodstream was saturated—the interior of Africa could be exploited by people of European descent.

If trade built the world economy, shipping, insurance, investment, and commissions provided additional means of stripping the undeveloped world of cash and commodities. Frequently, political control was only the final step in the increasing involvement of native peoples in the world economy and ultimately, their exploitation. The profits accruing to the West are an important part of the story, but so too is the human cost. From 1750 to 1913, Europe conquered 24 million square kilometers of African and Asian territory with a population of 534 million people. This assault cost approximately 300,000 European lives. Disease caused between two-thirds and three-quarters of those deaths. Between 800,000 and 1 million Africans and Asians died as a direct result of conquest. But the famines, forced migrations and other effects of European subjugation led to an estimated 25 million additional deaths. The rest of the world paid a series of heavy prices for the enrichment of Europeans and their descendants.[19]

LABOR AND IMPERIALISM

CHANGING CONDITIONS IN EUROPE

If the initial stages of the industrial revolution in Europe was predicated on the exploitation of the laboring classes, that situation did not endure unchanged or unchallenged. The responses of the people to extremely low wages, horrible working conditions, and harsh discipline varied widely from revolution, to machine-breaking, to the formation of unions, to emigration, to political lobbying.

After 1830, with noticeable bumps along the way like the "Hungry 1840s," the standard of living and political rights enjoyed by the laboring classes of Europe gradually improved. By 1852, a notoriously optimistic factory inspector could report: "I believe the workpeople never were so well off as they are at present; constant employment, good wages, cheap food, and cheap clothing; many cheap, innocent and elevating amusements brought within their reach; and ... time for some mental improvement, healthful recreation, and enjoyment of their friends and families."[20] Even in the more repressive

Published under the Authority of the SOCIETY *for
The Diffusion of* USEFUL KNOWLEDGE.

AN

ADDRESS

TO

THE LABOURERS,

ON THE

SUBJECT OF

DESTROYING MACHINERY.

LONDON:

PUBLISHED BY CHARLES KNIGHT,

PALL MALL EAST.

1830.

PRICE ONE PENNY,

With a Reduction to those who take a Quantity for distribution.

This widely circulated pamphlet entitled *Address to the Laborers on the Subject of Destroying Machinery* was published by the Society for the Diffusion of Useful Knowledge in 1830 as the fires of revolution burned across the Channel. Worried economic elites tried every tactic they could to convince workers that their exploitation was in their own best interest. The Society joined together a large number of large landowners and manufacturers. Machine-breaking was a major issue in England in 1829–1832. The Burndy Library, Cambridge, Massachusetts

European societies, growing profits from industry and the increased social and political weight of the working classes made it far more expedient to forestall revolution through concessions than to hope that repression would prevent revolution forever.

Beginning in the 1830s, legislation began to limit the exploitation of women and children in the mines and factories of Europe. Other laws regulated working conditions and the length of the work day. Political rights were also increasingly extended to many western European workers after the Revolutions of 1848. A limited ability to organize was also granted in some places; such rights expanded in the 1850s and 1860s. Although still subject to greater discipline and social control than other classes, many European workers recognized that their lives were improving, albeit too slowly for their taste. European workers' gains were, however, not mirrored in the colonies.

FEELING SUPERIOR

The emergence of a world economy permitted entrepreneurs to search out labor forces that were less organized, less militant, less powerful, and posed less of a physical threat to them than those at home. Europeans and their descendants had always treated other groups as inferior. Native populations were pushed aside all over the world to make way for European enterprise. The continuation of slavery during the critical decades of industrialization in the United Kingdom (abolished in 1833), France (1848), and the United States (1865) is a powerful indication of Western attitudes toward people of different backgrounds, but the opium trade foisted on China is no less revealing. Legal prohibitions and the looming "threat from below" made the exploitation of European workers less alluring to entrepreneurs. Neither condition applied to territories overseas inhabited by people of different races, creeds, and colors.

WAGE DISPARITIES

As was the case during the early phases of European industrialization, the search for the greatest possible profits or returns on invested capital led entrepreneurs to keep wages as low as possible. The wages paid to African laborers were generally kept *below* the poverty line; Africans were expected to grow food during their meager "leisure" time to supplement their earnings. The disparity between African and Western workers remained in place for decades, if not centuries. In the 1930s, a Nigerian coal miner at Enugu earned a shilling a day for underground work and 9 pence for surface jobs. A Scottish or German coal miner earned in an hour what a Nigerian earned in a week. Similar examples abound. In 1955, an American shipping company that transported goods between Africa and the United States paid five-sixths of the money to load and unload the ships to American workers. Yet the amount of cargo was the same at both ends and the trade ran in both directions. In late nineteenth-century and early twentieth-century Africa, the wages paid to an African varied from 16 to 25% of a European's (for the same work) in French North Africa to 10% in the mines and industries of the Rhodesias (present-day Zambia and Zimbabwe) and South Africa. The lower the wages, the more exceptional the profits earned by the Western corporations that had invested in African enterprises. Needless to say, the situation during the age of imperialism was not superior to that revealed by these more modern examples.[21]

RACISM AND EXPLOITATION

The explanations tendered by entrepreneurs and their defenders for why Africans or Asians received such low wages focused on their inferior technical skills, laziness, and lack of productivity. Similar arguments has been made for why the Irish received lower wages in English factories or for the minuscule percentage of male salaries garnered by women and children. To these long-standing polemical positions justifying low wages and high profits was added the issue of race.

Although legal slavery continued in parts of the Western Hemisphere until the 1890s and in large swaths of Africa and Asia until the twentieth century, slavery and contract labor were no longer efficient means of extracting the maximum amount of work for the lowest possible wages. Whereas it was in the best interest of slave-holders to keep their workforce healthy and productive, Europeans and their descendants created a global economic system in which they could pay Africans wages that fell well below the poverty line.

ACCEPTANCE?

Why did Africans and other colonized peoples accept this situation? This is not the place for a discussion of the administrative methods pioneered by the Europeans that pushed colonized people into the industrial labor force, but the impressive success of these methods meant that entrepreneurs in the colonies had ready access to a seemingly endless supply of unskilled labor. The ability of the colonial powers to maintain their exploitation across the decades was based on the monopoly of political power and superior armed forces developed by Europeans and their descendants. The concentration of workers in certain areas and in societies in general that made revolution a possibility in Europe did not exist in Africa and Asia where the working classes were small, dispersed and, in some areas, migratory.[22] Although the first stirrings of unrest came during the First World War, it was not until the Depression and then World War II which shattered the myth of Western invincibility that Africans and Asians began to reap the whirlwind of worker discontent in the European colonial empires.

Thomas Carlyle (1795–1881)
"Occasional Discourse on the Nigger Question" (1849)

Born in Scotland, Carlyle graduated from Edinburgh University and became a professional writer. His favored topic was leadership and its impact on political unrest as his most famous works: *The French Revolution* (1837); *On Heroes, Hero Worship and the Heroic in History* (1841); and *Past and Present* (1843) demonstrate. This offensive essay, initially published anonymously, but soon reprinted with Carlyle's name proudly affixed, was written in the aftermath of the Irish Potato Famine and the Revolutions of 1848. It came 15 years after the United Kingdom had outlawed slavery. The tone and language of Carlyle's observations about the need to force people of color in the West Indies to work like Europeans represent important and probably dominant views among British entrepreneurial elites.

no Black man who will not work according to what ability the gods have given him for working, has the smallest right to eat pumpkin [or any other food], or to any fraction of land that will grow pumpkin, however plentiful such land may be; but has an indisputable and perpetual *right* to be compelled, by the real proprietors of said land, to do competent work for his living ... Whatsoever prohibits or prevents a man from this his sacred appointment to labour while he lives on earth,—that, I say, is the man's deadliest enemy; and all men are called upon to do what is in their power or opportunity towards delivering him from that. If it be his own indolence that prevents and prohibits him, then his own indolence is the enemy he must be delivered from: and the first "right" he has,—poor indolent blockhead, black or white,—is, That every *un*prohibited man, whatsoever wiser, more industrious person may be passing that way, shall endeavor to "emancipate" him, since inducing will not serve, to do the work he is fit for. Induce him, if you can: yes, sure enough, by all means try what inducement will do; and indeed every coachman and carman knows that secret, without our preaching, and applies it to his horses as the true method: but if your Nigger will not be induced? In that case, it is full certain, he must be compelled; should and must; and the tacit prayer he makes (unconsciously he, poor blockhead), to you, and to me, and to all the world who are wiser than himself is, "Compel me!" For indeed he *must*, or else do and suffer worse,—he as well as we.

Source: Philip D. Curtin, ed., *Imperialism* (New York: Walker and Company, 1971), 141–42.

IMPERIALISM AND INDUSTRIALIZATION

The expansion of trade and the accompanying territorial acquisitions undertaken in the late fifteenth century by mercantilist European powers was the first, halting step toward a global economy. As trade and conquest blossomed in the sixteenth, seventeenth, and eighteenth centuries, a world trading system emerged. Only after the industrial revolution greatly widened the gap between Europe and other parts of the world did the global economy tilt inalterably toward the Western powers. By the mid-nineteenth century, the power differential had become a chasm too wide to bridge without shattering the political and military foundations of European economic domination.

The greatly heightened pace of colonial acquisition in the late nineteenth century was the result of advances in technology, industrial productivity, and social organization stemming from the industrial revolutions of the various Western powers.

The process by which the economic domination of Europe led to global political domination is marked by the persistent search for raw materials, new markets, and cheaper sources of labor. This process preceded industrialization by centuries, but the industrial revolution accelerated the phenomenon and allowed Europeans and their descendants in North America, South Africa, and Australia among other places to conquer and control vast territories more easily and cheaply than their ancestors could ever have dreamed. Improving conditions in Europe also encouraged entrepreneurs to look elsewhere for opportunities to maximize profits especially for the manufacture of goods capable of being produced by low-wage labor. Particularly in their colonial empires, the paternalistic good intentions trumpeted by many entrepreneurs were not realized in practice.

The exploitation of labor, native peoples, and entire regions by Europeans and their descendants were the cornerstones of their rapid acquisition of wealth. The military and economic power that resulted from technological advances and improvements in the organization of production created a gap between "the West and the rest" that enabled some groups to enrich themselves at the balance of the globe's expense. This distortion of global political economy allowed a prodigious and historically unprecedented increase in the wealth of Europeans and their descendants. Without the industrial revolutions experienced by the major colonial powers, Europe's position within the global economy would have been far less dominant and far less long-lived.

8

DEMAND, SUPPLY, AND THE FICKLE WHIMS OF FASHION

The interpretation of the industrial revolution presented in this book rejects many of the dominant views on the subject. Present-day explanations of the industrial revolution commonly focus on the role of an exogenous supply of new goods stemming from the creative genius of pioneering entrepreneurs and/or on the technological breakthroughs of dedicated tinkerers and scientists. Nearly all of the chief actors are British. The activities of these entrepreneurs and technologists created new objects that generated their own markets: if you make it, somebody will want to buy it. These fundamentally supply-side accounts do not reflect a broad look at the historical evidence which strongly favors a story of industrial development that has a place for the heroic entrepreneur and tinkerer, but recognizes that they were usually responding to needs or at least to a perceived demand. That said, however, the new goods produced during the industrial revolution—whether through a creative use of existing technologies or thanks to some sort of innovation in production—were crucial parts of industrialization. This chapter explores some of these new products and demonstrates that fashion, taste, and style can mediate the dictates of supply and demand.

EMULATION

More than a century before the industrial revolution, entrepreneurs recognized that the growing wealth of the various Western societies could be tapped by attractive or useful products and services. The higher wages and greater profits enjoyed by the many-layered middle classes and the more successful workers did not have to be saved or invested—this money could be spent. In the eighteenth century, one of the major innovations of industrialists like Josiah Wedgwood (see Chapter 4) was to adapt the strategies long used for attracting the custom of elites to the burgeoning middle classes. Kings, Queens, and high-ranking nobles were the pop singers, actors, and sports idols of their days: the ability to advertise wares as used by or supplied to "royalty" was a guarantee of quality and that the product was "fashionable" or "in style." In 1767, British author Nathaniel Forster observed: "a strong emulation in all the several stations and conditions [of society] to vie with each other; and the perpetual restless ambition in each of the inferior ranks to raise themselves to the level of those immediately above them. In such a state as this fashion must have uncontrolled sway. And a fashionable luxury must spread through it like a contagion."[1] Social emulation was an important part of the growing taste for luxury.

Other sources of goods to imitate came from abroad; in England, that usually meant France, India, or China. Indian calicos, Chinese silks and porcelain, and French clothing, fashion accessories, and luxury goods were all the rage in early industrial Britain. Changing tastes affect certain goods more rapidly than others. Selecting a housing style or foodstuffs is generally a more functional choice than choosing furniture or luxury items. One of the most changeable of consumer goods is clothing where fashionable shifts in texture, pattern, color, and stitching held great sway, especially as prices fell thanks to innovation. By the eighteenth century, even the laboring classes could afford stylish cloaks and shirts and began to wear muffs, nightclothes, and underwear. It is no accident that the emergence of the factory system and the industrial revolution itself focused on producing an exotic object of clothing first imported from India, cotton textiles.[2]

LUXURY

The application of the means and methods developed for the luxury market to other groups of consumers was a fundamental part of the increase in demand that preceded the industrial revolution. A major aim of eighteenth-century technological innovators and merchants was to render goods that had been luxuries into products that could be marketed to much wider audiences. This shift toward a wider market even within the luxury trade was a key link in the chain connecting demand and supply. In 1794, Matthew Boulton wrote to a fellow manufacturer: "We think it of far more consequence to supply the People than the Nobility only; and though you speak contemptuously of Hawkers, Pedlars and those who supply *Petty Shops*, yet we must own that we think they will do more towards supporting a great Manufactory, than all the Lords in the Nation."[3]

POPULUXE

The list of popularized luxuries ran the gamut from agricultural products such as tea, coffee, sugar, tobacco, and chocolate to manufactures like clocks, earthenware, cutlery, tea services, home furnishings, jewelry, watches, umbrellas, buckles, pins, glassware, and so forth. These goods, some useful and some decorative, have been termed "populuxe" for popular luxuries. They were developed for the sophisticated consumers of Paris and London and spread outward from there. Middle-class desires to acquire these objects stoked the fires of consumer demand and were crucial to the import substitution manufacturing strategies adopted by the mercantilist states of eighteenth and nineteenth century Europe (see Chapter 2). Such strategies were supported by the emerging nationalism of middle-class consumers: this trend was especially noteworthy in Britain.[4]

During the eighteenth century, this market began an almost exponential expansion as workers labored harder and for longer hours or used the wages garnered by their wives and children to afford some of these addictive status symbols (see Chapter 4). Patterns of acquisitiveness showed significant national and regional variations. A number of commentators believed that English workers preferred to acquire tangible goods. Their overfurnished homes contrasted with their undernourished bodies: those same commentators noted that French workers of similar relative income preferred to spend their money on food and drink. Others, like a British visitor to Paris in 1784 were surprised to encounter their milkman "dressed in a fashionable suit, with an embroidered waistcoat, silk knee-breeches and lace cuffs."[5]

The expansion of the consumer market down the social scale was a component of growing demand during the initial stages of the industrial revolution, but until the second half of the nineteenth century, increased purchasing by the middle classes was the chief element in the growth of demand. Before 1800, the popular classes focused on subsistence, only afterward did that pattern change, but when it did, consumption patterns changed rapidly. As industrial societies grew wealthier, this symbiotic process of increased consumer demand and enhanced ability to innovate helped the market's power to influence the allocation of resources evolve to new heights.

PRODUCT INNOVATION

Continual product innovation was essential to attracting the wandering eyes of fickle and wealthy consumers. The ability to innovate was a critical part of the process of innovation and marked a major divergence from the market environment of earlier eras where reliably made versions of standardized products, either by region or by a known manufacturer, were sold all over the globe. New dyes, fresh means of stitching, and the easy shifting of patterns via the Jacquard loom became available to textile manufacturers. The emergence of machine-tools permitted products made of metal to be varied constantly and simply. The explosion of choices allowed people to distinguish or differentiate themselves from others through their taste and style. The *Universal Magazine of Knowledge and Pleasure* appearing in 1772 pointed out that "all ranks of the people" engaged in this social contest through their "strong desire to signalise themselves in dress, equipage, houses, furniture, [and] amusements, etc."[6]

Reaching the Consumer

Speedier and more reliable modes of transportation, the reduction of transfer costs, and improved credit facilities facilitated the spread of "fashionable" goods. So too did innovative means of reaching the public. From traveling salesmen to showrooms in the capitals to printed catalogues and advertising in the growing number of "fashion" magazines that appeared in the 1770s throughout western Europe, merchants and manufacturers attempted to influence public taste. Entrepreneurs also developed goods that combined fashion (although not always good taste!) with trendiness. Medallions, ribbons, and even vases were engraved with contemporary messages that were sometimes political. Famous and occasionally infamous figures might also be represented.

Other merchants and manufacturers produced novelties or gadgets to stimulate jaded customers. These merchandising trends were significant departures from the more traditional approach where quality and sales were left to tend to themselves. A mid-nineteenth-century compilation of data on the Birmingham metal trades phrased the old situation like this: "The manufacturers remained at home and let the orders come to them." They were concerned with the "*making only.*"[7]

Shopping

This more passive conception of proper economic activity was superseded by innovative merchandisers and their suppliers who recognized the growing vogue for shopping as a leisure activity. With the easing of the religious strictures on luxury for groups other than elites dating from earlier eras, the middle classes embraced the pleasures of consumption. Enterprising merchants in upscale sections of cities where the well-off congregated created shops selling every imaginable luxury to catch the eye and empty the wallet. By concentrating on merchandising, certain thoroughfares or districts like Oxford Street in London or the rue St. Honoré in Paris became fashionable. Sophie von la Roche enthused: "Behind the great glass windows absolutely everything one can think of is neatly, attractively displayed, in such abundance of choice as almost to make one greedy. Now large slipper and shoe shops for anything from adults down to dolls, can be seen; now fashion-articles or silver or brass shops, books, guns, glasses, the confectioner's goodies, the pewterer's wares, fans."[8] To be seen there was part of the attraction, but consuming the tasteful displays was also part of the shopping experience. The emergence of a taste

This early nineteenth-century French vase was intended to be a collector's item. It is Greek in style
but has various masonic and revolutionary symbols
on it. The rubric: "From France to Lafayette" was
to honor this hero of the Revolutions of 1830,
1789, and the American Revolution. The Burndy
Library, Cambridge, Massachusetts

for luxury amongst middle-class consumers fostered the development of new
networks of experience linked to acquiring and displaying these fashionable
objects.

THE ROLE OF WOMEN

The role of women in the desire for   distinction and in the rise of shopping
as a social activity has been hotly debated. Women certainly were thoroughly
involved in the process of social differentiation. Shopping was a means of ex-
erting economic power and creating a market that catered to their needs and
desires. Women and men shopped for different things and were catered to
in disparate manners. Drinking tea was a feminine operation; women chose

As the first building constructed entirely of glass and steel, the Crystal Palace was itself a significant technical novelty. However, the three floors of displays became popular as a shopper's paradise. The Burndy Library, Cambridge, Massachusetts

the tea service and tea blends and oversaw both preparation and presentation. Men were responsible for "big ticket" furniture and housing decisions. Recent scholarly work suggests that although fashion, taste, style, and a preference for luxury could be coded as "feminine," the evidence is inconclusive. Maxine Berg argues that women experienced their possessions differently, especially clothing and decorative furnishings, but she reminds us that men were more involved in shopping than has been assumed by most economic models or by historians' examinations of the period.[9] Women were a fundamental part of the development of taste, fashion, style, and luxury, but both genders were responsible for the emergence of consumer capitalism.

EXPOSITIONS

Mercantile activity accelerated industrial creativity. Governments encouraged these efforts. Trade fairs were commonplace in much of commercial Europe, but these gatherings were oriented toward wholesale distribution more than retail sales. The French revolutionary government organized the first ever industrial exposition in 1798 as "an unknown means of amusement" to propagate the idea that only economic strength "can consolidate [the] victory [of French arms] and assure peace." Minister of the Interior

Nicholas-Louis François de Neufchâteau told the exhibitors that "You can fulfill a sacred duty by teaching the citizenry that national prosperity is inseparable from the health of the [mechanical] arts and manufacturing."[10] The significance of this consumer capitalism was increasingly apparent to all. Further French industrial expositions were held in 1801, 1802, 1806, 1819, 1823, 1827, 1834, 1839, 1841, 1844, and 1849. Numerous departments, cities, and regions held their own expositions when it became clear how useful these events were. Other countries, beginning with Austria in 1808, also got into the act. As discussed earlier, in 1851, the United Kingdom staged a version of the industrial exposition that combined the fair aspect with the presentation of international novelties and a shopping spectacle of unparalleled magnitude. The Crystal Palace exhibition is correctly known as the highpoint of English economic dominance and fashion ascendancy.

CONCLUSION

The industrial revolution transformed first European and then global society. This chapter has looked briefly at alterations in what and how people consumed. Thanks to industrialization, the objects that most Europeans and their descendants surrounded themselves with were far more decorative and far more numerous than had previously been the case. During this same period, how the middle classes and laborers spent their time—shopping, drinking tea, even taking into consideration the fickle whims of fashion—altered considerably, becoming recognizable to someone living today. Consumer capitalism is a fundamental part of the emergence of modernity in the Western world.

Creating this new economic environment extracted a grievous cost. Consumer capitalism was based on exploitation. Initially, the men, women, and children of the laboring classes of the industrializing world were the primary victims of the process. Even before the onset of industrialization, Europeans and their descendants had begun to exploit the people and resources of other parts of the world. The wealth garnered from the expansion of European power helped to jumpstart industrialization. The mistreatment, victimization, and expropriation of human beings, land and natural assets from non-Europeans accelerated during the industrial revolution. It peaked as industrial development and political evolution made it more difficult and less expedient to exploit the men, women, and children of Europeans and their descendants because of the fear of bloody revolution. The relative wealth of the Western world came, at least in part, from a long-term drain of other cultures in a process lasting centuries.

Even more concretely, the environment suffered heavy damage from coal smoke, strip mining, and chemical dumping. Finally, the coming of factory discipline altered the patriarchal and hierarchical relationships of European society. Consumer capitalism removed what the founding father of the political ideology of conservatism, the Anglo-Irish statesman Edmund Burke called, "All the pleasing illusions, which made power gentle, and obedience liberal, which harmonized the different shades of life."[11] Industrial society was more individualistic, more profit-oriented, and more unsettled both regarding an individual's place in the universe and in their community.

THE NAPOLEONIC WATERSHED

This nineteenth-century shift in the nature of Western society took place in an altered political and administrative environment. The post-1815 regimes of Europe had more modern means to engage in wealth-making in industry at their disposal because of the efforts undertaken to defeat Napoleon. Every state apparatus had greater capacity to enhance the supply of crucial economic indicators and thus to strengthen and broaden demand than their eighteenth-century forebears. Although little seems to have changed before and after the Napoleonic challenge, this appearance is misleading. Administratively, as shown in Chapter 7, the governments of Europe were poised to take an ever greater economic role no matter what lip service they paid to the concept of "laissez-faire, laissez-passer."

NEW SALES METHODS

As the global economy came into being and urban markets developed, entrepreneurs now had new ways of making and selling goods. Profits could come from innovative manufacturing processes in all the ways explored in Chapters 3 and 4. Traditionally made products could be sold in different places or in new ways. Employing traveling salesmen, advertising, and using shop presentation to make their wares appear more fashionable, more luxurious, and more in-style were also dared.

As price-fixing and limitations on production disappeared, competition became the watchword of industry, forcing entrepreneurs who wanted to maintain or increase profits to experiment and explore in ways that marked the dawn of the modern business environment.

The new business climate made entrepreneurialism both more difficult and more necessary. As the choices and options multiplied, so too did the possibilities of failure. Outrageous profits were possible, but only to the innovative. Steady, limited profits were also to be found, but discovering the degree of change needed to keep up in a rapidly changing business environment was extremely difficult, especially considering the uncertain knowledge of conditions and the deeply flawed managerial and accounting tools available. Successful industrial entrepreneurs *were* heroic, but heroism did not translate directly to

This trial vehicle operated by the London & Paddington Steam Carriage Company in the early 1830s was named after the deity of industrial Britain and late twentieth century America: the "Enterprise." Fashionably dressed ladies and gentlemen took their chances aboard this technologically precocious conveyance decorated with imperialistic designs. The Burndy Library, Cambridge, Massachusetts

success. Bankruptcies and other forms of failure were far more common fates for the innovator than long-term success. "Enterprise" became the essential business goal, but effective planning, implementing, and managing any and all changes would only come with the Second Industrial Revolution[12] that began at the tail end of the nineteenth century.

GLOSSARY

Apprenticeship. A system of training young skilled laborers that was relatively formalized by the guilds of Europe.

Bourbon (House of). Ruling dynasty of France 1589–1793, 1814–1830. Other branches of the family ruled or rule southern Italy and Spain.

Capital/Capital stock. An element of production from which income is derived: land and labor are exempted. Here the usage refers to financial capital rather than other marketable intangibles like good will. Capital stock should be understood as circulating capital as opposed to fixed capital such as machines, buildings, or tools.

Coke. The solid residue of coal that has been baked rather than burned.

Commodity. Something capable of being sold. Here it does not refer to anything that can be bought and sold, but rather commodities are used to denote primary goods: those things produced by agriculture, mining, forestry, and fishing.

Customs. See tariff.

Enclosure. The process by which land that had been subject to common rights including fields, waste, and pasture was fenced in for private use.

Fertility. In demography, fertility refers to the number of children born.

Foreign trade. Traffic in goods conducted by gift, barter, or sale with other political entities. Trade with overseas dependencies counts as domestic trade.

Gross National Product (GNP). The total value of new, final goods and services produced in a year by inhabitants of a country. It includes income from investments and activities undertaken abroad. Final goods and services means that they are consumed, not used to produce something else. The proper means of calculating GNP is deeply contested.

Guild. An association of people with the same skill or craft. In Europe, the guilds produced certain goods under a monopoly for a particular urban area granted by higher authorities. They guaranteed quality, protected mutual interests, and regulated labor.

Hanover (House of). Ruling dynasty of Great Britain and the United Kingdom since 1714.

Jacobite. Supporter of the House of Stuart ousted by the Glorious Revolution in England. The Jacobites rose in rebellion in 1715 and 1745.

Joint-stock company. In this form of business organization, the profits and losses of the company created by the capital invested by the stockholders is shared outproportionately according to their stake.

Justice of the Peace (JP). In the English legal system, this local official was a representative of the central state with significant administrative and police powers. Until the late nineteenth century, they had judicial jurisdiction over most crimes.

National income. The total value of all income within a nation or by its citizens including wages, profits, rents, interest and pensions.

Nuptuality. In demography, nuptuality refers to the proportion of adults who marry.

Paternalism. Literally referring to the authority of a male parent, it is often seen as a negative attribute of state regulation. In origin, paternalism was intended to safeguard the objects of oversight from exploitation, poor choices or such things as accidents and disasters.

Poor Law. In England, the legislation dealing with public assistance for the poor was passed in 1601. A century later, workhouses were created and supported by local dues levied on the parish. The poor were expected to labor and apprenticeships were also provided for children. The system was revised thoroughly in 1834.

Pound, shilling, pence. Denominations of the currency of England, then Great Britain and finally the United Kingdom. There are 12 pence (d.) in a shilling (s.) and 20 shillings in a pound (£). In 1850, the exchange rate was $4.87 to £1.

Productivity. Refers to the output of any means of production per unit of input. Increasing productivity is a major factor in generating economic growth.

Real wages. This measure refers to the payments received by an employee for their labor. It refers both to salaried and hourly wage-earners. Real wages is a measure that discounts wages for inflation to permit meaningful comparisons.

Re-export. The re-export of goods refers to sending of products received from one source to another destination. It is also applies to shipping goods produced by colonies to third parties.

Standard of living. This index refers to the level of consumption achieved by an individual, group, or nation. It is a relative index based on the cost of living and the wage scales of those involved. Discretionary income and access to goods and services are important indicators of the standard of living.

Tariff. Tax on imported and sometimes on exported goods. The revenue is generally collected at the frontiers by a customs service. The tariff can impose a flat rate on all imported or exported goods or it can be targeted to specific items.

Utopian socialism. This brand of socialism emphasized that the production and distribution of goods should be handled by the state. Its chief figures included the Count of Saint-Simon, Charles Fourier, and Robert Owen. Instead of focusing on the struggle between classes, they wanted to create a national community based on cooperation that would eliminate poverty.

NOTES

CHAPTER 1

1. The place names of the British Isles are confusing. England is a country that is found on the southern three-quarters of the eastern island. Scotland is to the north. "England" will refer only to that region. Great Britain is the name of the country formed by the union of England (which controlled Wales and Ireland) and Scotland in 1707. When Ireland was admitted as a partner in 1801 the name of the union was the United Kingdom.

2. T.S. Ashton, *The Industrial Revolution 1760–1830*, revised ed. (London: Oxford University Press, 1969 [1948]), 42, 66, and 98.

3. On this controversial point, see Joseph E. Inikori, *Africans and the Industrial Revolution in England: A Study in International Trade and Economic Development* (Cambridge: Cambridge University Press, 2002) and Jeff Horn, *The Path Not Taken: French Industrialization in the Age of Revolution 1750–1830* (Cambridge, MA: MIT Press, 2006).

4. Roderick Floud and Paul Johnson, eds., *The Cambridge Economic History of Modern Britain, Vol. 1: Industrialisation, 1700–1860* (Cambridge: Cambridge University Press, 2004), 4, 6, 186–87, 323, and 460, and Leandro Prados de la Escosura, ed., *Exceptionalism and Industrialisation: Britain and Its European Rivals, 1688–1815* (Cambridge: Cambridge University Press, 2004), 261.

5. Maxine Berg, *The Age of Manufactures 1700–1820: Industry, Innovation and Work in Britain*, 2nd ed. (London: Routledge, 1994), 138.

6. Floud and Johnson, eds., *The Cambridge Economic History of Modern Britain*, 91–92 and 200, Phyllis Deane and W.A. Cole, *British Economic Growth 1688–1959: Trends and Structure*, 2nd ed. (Cambridge: Cambridge University Press, 1967), 212, and Inikori, *Africans and the Industrial Revolution in England*, 75–78 and 85.

7. Floud and Johnson, eds., *The Cambridge Economic History of Modern Britain*, 57–95.

8. Ibid., 5, 272–73, 291, and 292.

9. The previous two paragraphs are based on Floud and Johnson, eds., *The Cambridge Economic History of Modern Britain*, 263, 268–94.

10. All quotations in the succeeding paragraphs are from Robert Owen, "Observations on the Effect of the Manufacturing System, 1815" reprinted in G.D.H. Cole and A.W. Filson, eds., *British Working Class Movements: Select Documents 1789–1875* (New York: St. Martin's Press, 1967), 8–11.

CHAPTER 2

1. Arthur Young, *General Report on Enclosures (1808)*, 219, cited in Martin J. Daunton, *Progress and Poverty: An Economic and Social History of Britain 1700–1850* (Oxford: Oxford University Press, 1995), 113.

2. Young, *General Report on Enclosures*, 220, cited in Daunton, *Progress and Poverty*, 114.

3. Jan DeVries, "Between Purchasing Power and the World of Goods: Understanding the Household Economy in Early Modern Europe," in John Brewer and Roy Porter, eds., *Consumption and the World of Goods* (London: Routledge, 1994), 85–132 and idem, "The Industrial Revolution and the Industrious Revolution," *The Journal of Economic History*, 54(2) (June 1994), 249–70. The quote is from 255.

4. Neil McKendrick, "The Consumer Revolution of Eighteenth Century England," in Neil McKendrick, John Brewer, and J.H. Plumb, *The Birth of a Consumer Society: The Commercialization of Eighteenth-Century England* (Bloomington: Indiana University Press, 1982), 9–33.

5. Sidney W. Mintz, "The Changing Roles of Food in the Study of Consumption," in John Brewer and Roy Porter, eds., *Consumption and the World of Goods* (London: Routledge, 1994), 261–73.

6. James Stueart, *An Inquiry into the Principles of Political Economy*, 67 (1767) cited by DeVries, "The Industrial Revolution and the Industrious Revolution," 259.

7. Adam Smith, *The Wealth of Nations*, intro Robert Reich (New York: Modern Library, 2000 [1776]), 20, Book I, Chapter 3.

8. Daunton, *Progress and Poverty*, 288.

9. Roderick Floud and Paul Johnson, eds., *The Cambridge Economic History of Modern Britain*, 299.

10. Floud and Johnson, eds., *The Cambridge Economic History of Modern Britain*, 322.

11. Ralph Davis, *The Rise of the English Shipping Industry in the Seventeenth and Eighteenth Centuries* (1962), cited by Daunton, *Progress and Poverty*, 294.

12. Floud and Johnson, eds., *The Cambridge Economic History of Modern Britain*, 322.

13. Peter Mathias, *The First Industrial Nation: An Economic History of Britain 1700–1914*, 2nd ed. (London: Routledge, 1983 [1969]), 104.

14. Floud and Johnson, eds., *The Cambridge Economic History of Modern Britain*, 297, 299.

15. Floud and Johnson, eds., *The Cambridge Economic History of Modern Britain*, 322.

16. Inikori, *Africans and the Industrial Revolution*, 202.

17. Inikori, *Africans and the Industrial Revolution*, 181, 197.

18. Deane and Cole, *British Economic Growth 1688–1959*, 48 and Mathias, *The First Industrial Nation*, 88–89.

19. Mathias, *The First Industrial Nation*, 86.

20. Philippe Minard, *La fortune du colbertisme: État et industrie dans la France des Lumières* (Paris: Fayard, 1998), 194. The translation is mine.

21. Cited by J.L. Hammond and Barbara Hammond, *The Skilled Labourer 1760–1832* (New York: Harper Torchbooks, 1970 [1919]), 50.

22. Denis Woronoff, *Histoire de l'Industrie en France du XVIe siècle à nos jours* (Paris: Seuil, 1994), 81.

23. William M. Reddy, *The Rise of Market Culture: The Textile Trade & French Society, 1750–1900* (Cambridge and Paris: Cambridge University Press and Éditions de la Maison des Sciences de l'Homme, 1984), 31.

24. Patrick Verley, *La Révolution industrielle* (Paris: Gallimard, 1997), 409.

25. Floud and Johnson, eds., *The Cambridge Economic History of Modern Britain*, 185, 188.

26. Unless otherwise noted British tax statistics come from Ron Harris, "Government and the Economy, 1688–1850," in Floud and Johnson, eds., *The Cambridge Economic History of Modern Britain*, 204–37, and Patrick O'Brien, "Central Government and the Economy, 1688–1815," in Roderick Floud and Donald McCloskey, eds., *The Economic History of Britain since 1700, Vol. 1: 1700–1860*, 2nd ed. (Cambridge: Cambridge University Press, 1994), 205–41.

27. Quoted in Roy Porter, *English Society in the Eighteenth Century*, revised ed. (London: Penguin Books, 1990 [1982]), 117–18.

CHAPTER 3

1. Quoted in Paul Mantoux, *The Industrial Revolution in the Eighteenth Century: An Outline of the Beginnings of the Modern Factory System in England* (New York: Harper & Row, 1961), 203.

2. Kenneth Morgan, *The Birth of Industrial Britain: Economic Change 1750–1850* (London: Longman, 1999), 41–42.

3. Roderick Floud and Paul Johnson, eds., *The Cambridge Economic History of Modern Britain*, 429.

4. Cited by J.R. Harris, *Industrial Espionage and Technology Transfer: Britain and France in the Eighteenth Century* (Aldershot: Ashgate, 1998), 36–37.

5. Floud and Johnson, eds., *The Cambridge Economic History of Modern Britain*, 429, and Berg, *The Age of Manufactures 1700–1820*, 45.

6. Ken Alder, *Engineering the Revolution: Arms and Enlightenment in France, 1763–1815* (Princeton: Princeton University Press, 1997), 221–51, 321–23, and Charles Coulston Gillispie, *Science and Polity in France: The Revolutionary and Napoleonic Years* (Princeton: Princeton University Press, 2004), 424–26.

7. Pauline Maier, Merritt Roe Smith, Alexander Keyssar, and Daniel J. Kevles, *Inventing America: A History of the United States* (New York: W.W. Norton & Co., 2003), 274–75, and David S. Landes, *Revolution in Time: Clocks and the Making of the Modern World*, revised ed. (Cambridge, MA: Belknap Press, 2000 [1983]), 336.

CHAPTER 4

1. Paul Mantoux, *The Industrial Revolution in the Eighteenth Century: An Outline of the Beginnings of the Modern Factory System in England* (New York: Harper & Row, 1961), 224–25.

2. Letter published in the *Manchester Mercury* on October 12, 1779. Reproduced in Mantoux, *The Industrial Revolution in the Eighteenth Century*, 402.

3. Thomas Young made this assertion in 1807. Quoted in Charles Singer, E.J. Holmyard, A.R. Hall and Trevor I. Williams, *A History of Technology, Vol. IV: The Industrial Revolution c1750 to c1850* (New York: Oxford University Press, 1958), 164.

4. Cited by J.L. Hammond and Barbara Hammond, *The Rise of Modern Industry* (London: Methuen, 1966 [1925]), 127.

5. Charles Singer, et al., *A History of Technology*, 163.

6. Kenneth Morgan, *The Birth of Industrial Britain: Economic Change 1750–1850* (London: Longman, 1999), 40.

7. Roderick Floud and Paul Johnson, eds., *The Cambridge Economic History of Modern Britain, Vol. 1: Industrialisation, 1700–1860* (Cambridge: Cambridge University Press, 2004), 37.

8. Cited in Sidney Pollard, *The Genesis of Modern Management: A Study of the Industrial Revolution in Great Britain* (Cambridge: Harvard University Press, 1965), 122.

9. Quoted in Peter Mathias, *The Transformation of England: Essays in the Economic and Social History of England in the Eighteenth Century* (London: Methuen, 1979), 226–27.

10. The previous two paragraphs are based on Peter Mathias, *The First Industrial Nation: An Economic History of Britain 1700–1914*, 2nd ed. (London: Routledge, 1983 [1969]), 119, 132, and 134.

11. Maxin Berg, *The Age of Manufactures 1700–1820: Industry, Innovation and Work in Britain*, 2nd ed. (London: Routledge, 1994), 195.

12. Edwin Cannan, ed., *Adam Smith: The Wealth of Nations* (New York: Modern Library, 2000 [1776]), Book I, Chapter 1.

13. Berg, *The Age of Manufactures*, 141.

14. John Rule, *The Labouring Classes in Early Industrial England 1750–1850* (London: Longman, 1986), 15.

15. Pollard, *The Genesis of Modern Management*, 189.

16. Cited by Hammond and Hammond, *The Rise of Modern Industry*, 199.

17. Cited by J.L. Hammond and Barbara Hammond, *The Town Labourer: The New Civilization, 1760–1832* (Garden City, NJ: Anchor Books, 1968 [1920]), 133.

18. Morgan, *The Birth of Industrial Britain*, 43.

19. Hammond and Hammond, *The Town Labourer*, 140.

20. From J. Smith, *Memoirs of Wool* (1747), cited by E.P. Thompson, *The Making of the English Working Class* (New York: Vintage Books, 1963), 277.

21. Cited by Roy Porter, *English Society in the Eighteenth Century*, revised ed. (London: Penguin Books, 1990 [1982]), 326.

22. Hammond and Hammond, *The Town Labourer*, 17–18.

23. These are Arkwright's words. Cited by Pollard, *The Genesis of Modern Management*, 183.

24. Smith, *The Wealth of Nations*, 840, Book V, Chapter 1, Part III.

25. Hammond and Hammond, *The Town Labourer*, 257–58.

26. Kevin Binfield, ed., *Writings of the Luddites* (Baltimore: the Johns Hopkins University Press, 2004), 72–73.

27. Cited by J.L. and Barbara Hammond and Hammond, *The Skilled Labourer 1760–1832* (New York: Harper Torchbooks, 1970 [1919]), 59–60.

28. Cited by Thompson, *The Making of the English Working Class*, 329.

29. Ibid., 330–31.

CHAPTER 5

1. Roderick Floud and Paul Johnson, *The Cambridge Economic History of Modern Britain, Vol. 1: Industrialisation, 1700–1860* (Cambridge: Cambridge University Press, 2004), 96 and Steven King and Geoffrey Timmons, *Making Sense of the Industrial Revolution: English Economy and Society 1700–1850* (Manchester: Manchester University Press, 2001), 165.

2. Patrick O'Brien, "Deconstructing the British Industrial Revolution as a Conjuncture and Paradigm for Global Economic History," in Jeff Horn, Leonard N. Rosenband, and Merritt Roe Smith, eds., *Reconceptualizing the Industrial Revolution* (Cambridge, MA: MIT Press, 2007), forthcoming.

3. Ian Inkster and Patrick O'Brien, eds., "The Global History of the Steam Engine," *History of Technology* 25, Special Issue (2004), cited by O'Brien, "Deconstructing."

4. Floud and Johnson, *The Cambridge Economic History of Modern Britain*, 422, 429.

5. Leandro Prados de la Escosura, ed., *Exceptionalism and Industrialisation: Britain and Its European Rivals, 1688–1815* (Cambridge: Cambridge University Press, 2004), 62, and Phyllis Deane and W.A. Cole, *British Economic Growth 1688–1959: Trends and Structure*, 2nd ed. (Cambridge: Cambridge University Press, 1967), 44.

6. I rely on the work of Patrick O'Brien for this interpretation. See O'Brien, "Deconstructing," "Central Government and the Economy, 1688–1815," in Floud and McCloskey, eds., *The Economic History of Britain since 1700*, 205–41, and "Political Preconditions for the Industrial Revolution," in Patrick O'Brien and Roland Quinault, eds., *The Industrial Revolution and British Society* (Cambridge: Cambridge University Press, 1993), 124–55. This theme is taken up and expanded on powerfully in Prados de la Escosura, ed., *Exceptionalism and Industrialisation*.

7. E.P. Thompson, *The Making of the English Working Class* (New York: Vintage Books, 1963), 605.

8. Patrick Colquhoun, *Treatise on the Wealth, Power and Resources of the British Empire* (1814), cited by O'Brien, "Political preconditions," 128.

9. These historians include O'Brien, Martin Daunton, *Progress and Poverty: An Economic and Social History of Britain 1700–1850* (Oxford: Oxford University Press, 1995), 477–502, Richard Price, *British Society 1680–1880: Dynamism, Containment and Change* (Cambridge: Cambridge University Press, 1999), and William

J. Ashworth, *Consuming the People: Trade, Production, and the English Customs and Excise 1643–1842* (Oxford: Oxford University Press, 2003).

10. Joel Mokyr, *The Lever of Riches. Technological Creativity and Economic Progress* (New York: Oxford University Press, 1990), 294.

11. Cited by Margaret C. Jacob, *Scientific Culture and the Making of the Industrial West* (New York: Oxford University Press, 1997), 110.

CHAPTER 6

1. Kenneth Pomeranz, *The Great Divergence: China, Europe, and the Making of the Modern World Economy* (Princeton: Princeton University Press, 2000).

2. Herbinot de Mauchamps, ed., *Mémoires de M. Richard-Lenoir* (Paris: Delaunay, 1837), 264.

3. Richard J. Barker, "The Conseil général des Manufactures under Napoleon (1810–1814)," *French Historical Studies* 6(2) (Fall 1969), 188.

4. Charles Sabel and Jonathan Zeitlin, "Historical Alternatives to Mass Production: Politics, Markets and Technology in Nineteenth-Century Industrialization," *Past and Present* 108 (1985), 133–76.

5. Jean-Charles Asselain, *Histoire économique de la France du XVIIIE siècle à nos jours, Vol 1: De l'Ancien Régime à la Première Guerre mondiale* (Paris: Seuil, 1984), 130, Patrick Verley, *La Révolution industrielle* (Paris: Gallimard, 1997), 317, Maurice Lévy-Leboyer, "Capital Investment and Economic Growth in France, 1820–1930," in Peter Mathias and M. M. Postan, eds., *The Cambridge Economic History of Europe* VII (1), *The Industrial Economies: Capital, Labour, and Enterprise: Britain, France, Germany, and Scandinavia* (Cambridge: Cambridge University Press, 1978), 267, and Jean-Pierre Daviet, *La société industrielle en France 1814–1914: Productions, échanges, représentations* (Paris: Seuil, 1997), 17.

6. Philip T. Hoffman and Jean-Laurent Rosenthal, "New Work in French Economic History," *French Historical Studies* 23(3) (2000), 451, Christian Morrisson and Wayne Snyder, "The income inequality of France in historical perspective," *European Review of Economic History* 4 (2000), 72, and François Crouzet, *Britain Ascendant: Comparative Studies in Franco-British Economic History*, trans. Martin Thom (Cambridge and Paris: Cambridge University Press and Éditions de la Maison des Sciences de l'Homme, 1990), 342.

7. Alfred D. Chandler Jr., *The Visible Hand: The Managerial Revolution in American Business* (Cambridge, MA: Belknap Press, 1977), 58–59.

8. David J. Jeremy, *Transatlantic Industrial Revolution: The Diffusion of Textile Technologies Between Britain and America, 1790–1830s* (Cambridge: the MIT Press, 1981), 190.

9. Peter Temin, *Engines of Enterprise: An Economic History of New England* (Cambridge: Harvard University Press, 2000), 100.

10. Phyllis Deane and W.A. Cole, *British Economic Growth 1688–1959: Trends and Structure*, 2nd ed. (Cambridge: Cambridge University Press, 1967), 103.

11. Robert H. Baird, *The American Cotton Spinner and Managers' and Carders' Guide: A Practical Treatise on Cotton Spinning: Giving the Dimensions and Speed of Machinery, Draught and Twist Calculations, etc., with Notices of Recent Improvements, Together with Rules and Examples for Making Changes in the Size and Numbers of*

Roving and Yarn (Philadelphia: Henry Carey Baird, 1863), 20. http://resolver. library.cornell.edu/hoec/4088776 (July 2006).

12. Brooke Hindle and Steven Lubar, *Engines of Change: The American Industrial Revolution 1790–1860* (Washington, DC: Smithsonian Institute Press, 1986), 228, and Pauline Maier, Merritt Roe Smith, Alexander Keyssar, and Daniel J. Kevles, *Inventing America: A History of the United States* (New York: W.W. Norton, 2003), 322.

13. David S. Landes, *The Wealth and Poverty of Nations: Why Some Are So Rich and Some Are So Poor* (New York: W.W. Norton, 1998), 303–4.

14. Hindle and Lubar, *Engines of Change*, 79.

15. Maier, Smith, Keyssar, and Kevles, *Inventing America*, 308.

16. Ibid., 352.

17. Judith A. McGaw, *Most Wonderful Machine: Mechanization and Social Change in Berkshire Paper Making 1801–1885* (Princeton: Princeton University Press, 1987), 121.

18. McGaw, *Most Wonderful Machine*, 128, 250.

19. On this trend, see the influential argument of Chandler, *The Visible Hand* and for an example, see McGaw, *Most Wonderful Machine*, Chapter 5.

20. H.J. Habakkuk and M. Postan, eds., *The Cambridge Economic History of Europe, Vol. VI, Part II: The Industrial Revolutions and After: Incomes, Population and Technological Change* (Cambridge: Cambridge University Press, 1965), 681–83, and Chandler, *The Visible Hand*, 76.

21. Maier, Smith, Keyssar, and Kevles, *Inventing America*, 466–68.

22. Cited in Eric Dorn Brose, *The Politics of Technological Change in Prussia: Out of the Shadow of Antiquity, 1809–1848* (Princeton: Princeton University Press, 1993), 68.

23. Mathias and Postan, eds., *The Cambridge Economic History of Europe*, VII(1), 534.

24. Joel Mokyr, *Industrialization in the Low Countries, 1795–1850* (New Haven, CT: Yale University Press, 1976), 60.

25. Cited in W.O. Henderson, *The Industrial Revolution in Europe: Germany, France, Russia, 1815–1914* (Chicago: Quadrangle Books, 1968 [1961]), 30.

26. Eric Dorn Brose, "The Political Economy of Early Industrialization in German Europe, 1800–1840," in Jeff Horn, Leonard N. Rosenband, and Merritt Roe Smith, eds., *Reconceptualizing the Industrial Revolution* (Cambridge: MIT Press, 2007), forthcoming, Henderson, *The Industrial Revolution in Europe*, 19, and Peter Mathias, and M. Postan, eds., *The Cambridge Economic History of Europe, Vol. VII: The Industrial Economies: Capital Labour, and Enterprise, Part I, Britain, France, Germany, and Scandinavia* (Cambridge: Cambridge University Press, 1978), 414.

27. Henderson, *The Industrial Revolution in Europe*, 21–24, and Carlo M. Cipolla, ed., *The Emergence of Industrial Societies*, Vol. 4, Part 1 of *The Fontana Economic History of Europe* (Bath: Harvester Press, 1973), 123.

28. W.O. Henderson, *The State and the Industrial Revolution in Prussia 1740–1870* (Liverpool: Liverpool University Press, 1958), xvii.

29. Henderson, *The State and the Industrial Revolution*, 31–32, 34–36, Brose, "The Political Economy of Early Industrialization," and H.J. Habakkuk and M. Postan, eds., *The Cambridge Economic History of Europe, Vol. VI, Part I: The Industrial*

Revolutions and After: Incomes, Population and Technological Change (Cambridge: Cambridge University Press, 1965), 17, Mathias, and Postan, eds., *The Cambridge Economic History of Europe*, VII (1), 472.

30. Carlo M. Cipolla, ed., *The Emergence of Industrial Societies*, Vol. 4, Part 2 of *The Fontana Economic History of Europe* (Bath: Harvester Press, 1973), 770, 773.

31. Sidney Pollard, *Peaceful Conquest: The Industrialization of Europe 1760–1970* (New York: Oxford University Press, 1981), 92–93.

CHAPTER 7

1. H.L. Wesserling, *The European Colonial Empires, 1815–1919*, trans. Diane Webb (Harlow, United Kingdom: Pearson/Longman, 2004), 13. The 2000 figure is that reported by the United Nations Council on Population.

2. Mark Kishlansky, Patrick Geary, and Patricia O'Brien, *Civilization in the West*, 5th ed. (New York: Longman, 2003), 829.

3. Wesserling, *The European Colonial Empires*, 29.

4. T.O. Lloyd, *The British Empire 1558–1983* (Oxford: Oxford University Press, 1984), 401, and J. Holland Rose, A.P. Newton, and E.A. Benians, *The Growth of the New Empire 1783–1870*, Vol. II of *The Cambridge History of the British Empire* (Cambridge: Cambridge University Press, 1961), 778.

5. Sumit Sankar, *Modern India 1885–1947* (Madras: Macmillan, 1983), 39, Wesserling, *The European Colonial Empires*, 25, and Carlo M. Cipolla, ed., *The Emergence of Industrial Societies*, Vol. 4 of *The Fontana Economic History of Europe* (Brighton, United Kingdom: Harvester Press, 1973), 670.

6. Sankar, *Modern India*, 25, 27.

7. Rose, Newton, and Benians, *The Growth of the New Empire*, 400–401.

8. Ibid., 778.

9. Stanley Wolpert, *A New History of India*, 4th ed. (New York: Oxford University Press, 1993), 259.

10. Wolpert, *A New History of India*, 230, 243, and Wesserling, *The European Colonial Empires*, 30.

11. Cited by Daniel R. Headrick, *The Tools of Empire: Technology and European Imperialism in the Nineteenth Century* (New York: Oxford University Press, 1981), 180.

12. Wolpert, *A New History of India*, 267, and Rose, Newton, and Benians, *The Growth of the New Empire*, 771.

13. Cipolla, ed., *The Emergence of Industrial Societies*, 659, 666.

14. Eric J. Hobsbawm, *Industry and Empire: From 1750 to the Present Day*, with Chris Wrigley (New York: the New Press, 1999 [1968]), 113, and Cipolla, ed., *The Emergence of Industrial Societies*, 658, 669.

15. Hobsbawm, *Industry and Empire*, 116–17, and Wesserling, *The European Colonial Empires*, 27.

16. Walter Rodney, *How Europe Underdeveloped Africa* (Washington, DC: Howard University Press, 1982), 136.

17. Wesserling, *The European Colonial Empires*, 27, and Hobsbawm, *Industry and Empire*, 118, 123.

18. Cipolla, ed., *The Emergence of Industrial Societies*, 694, and Hobsbawm, *Industry and Empire*, 123.

19. Wesserling, *The European Colonial Empires*, 32, 34.

20. G.M. Young and W.D. Handcock, eds., *English Historical Documents 1833–1894* (New York: Oxford University Press, 1956), 902.

21. Rodney, *How Europe Underdeveloped Africa*, 149–52.

22. These observations are based on Rodney, *How Europe Underdeveloped Africa*, 150. Although Rodney's conclusions are controversial, his evidence of the continuing exploitation of Africans is convincing.

CHAPTER 8

1. Quoted in Neil McKendrick, John Brewer, and J.H. Plumb, *The Birth of a Consumer Society: The Commercialization of Eighteenth-Century England* (Bloomington: Indiana University Press, 1982), 11.

2. Carlo M. Cipolla, ed., *The Industrial Revolution*, Vol. 3 of *The Fontana Economic History of Europe* (Glasgow: Fontanta/Collins, 1973), 96–97.

3. Quoted in McKendrick, Brewer, and Plumb, *The Birth of a Consumer Society*, 77.

4. Cissie Fairchilds, "The Production and Marketing of Populuxe Goods in Eighteenth-Century Paris," in John Brewer and Roy Porter, eds., *Consumption and the World of Goods* (London: Routledge, 1993), 228–48. See also the insights from the editors, together and singly in Maxine Berg and Helen Clifford, *Consumers and Luxury: Consumer Culture in Europe 1650–1850* (Manchester: Manchester University Press, 1999), 6, 65 and Maxine Berg, *Luxury & Pleasure in Eighteenth-Century Britain* (Oxford: Oxford University Press, 2005), 7–8.

5. Cipolla, ed., *The Industrial Revolution*, 154, and Fairchilds, "The Production and Marketing of Populuxe Goods," 228.

6. This point and these quotations are from Berg, *Luxury & Pleasure*, 4.

7. Cipolla, ed., *The Industrial Revolution*, 141, and McKendrick, Brewer, and Plumb, *The Birth of a Consumer Society*, 67. The italics are in the original cited here.

8. Cited by McKendrick, Brewer, and Plumb, *The Birth of a Consumer Society*, 79.

9. See Berg, *Luxury & Pleasure*, 234–46.

10. The quotations are from the *Réimpression de l'Ancien Moniteur* 29:1 (Paris: Imprimerie Nationale, 1847), September 26, 1798, 402–3.

11. Burke was referring to the political innovations of the French Revolution, but his analysis fits the Industrial Revolution at least as well. Edmund Burke, *Reflections on the Revolution in France* was published in 1790. For a hypertext version, see: http://www.constitution.org/eb/rev_fran.htm (Consulted July 2006).

12. A number of distinguished historians reject the notion of a Second Industrial Revolution in the manner best described by David Landes in *The Unbound Prometheus*. See Jan DeVries, "Economic Growth Before and After the Industrial Revolution," in Maarten Prak, ed., *Early Modern Capitalism: Economic and Social Change in Europe 1400–1800* (London: Routledge, 2001), 177–94. To my way of thinking, the changes in communications, managerial practices, the emergence of large-scale corporations, the use of refrigeration, the growth of different energy sources such as petroleum, along with the development of urban transportation networks and the labor environment represent a revolutionary transformation. Thus, the term "Second Industrial Revolution" denotes something unique and important.

A NOTE ON SOURCES

The industrial revolution is a complex, international story that stretches across centuries. As we have seen, however, it started in Great Britain. A set of important studies of the British industrial revolution were published in the 1960s that still set much of the agenda for exploring this important subject. E.P. Thompson, *The Making of the English Working Class* (New York: Vintage Books, 1963) is the towering figure of modern labor history. Reading this book will give a real sense of the problems and challenges faced by the working classes during the later stages of the industrial revolution. Sidney Pollard, *The Genesis of Modern Management: A Study of the Industrial Revolution in Great Britain* (Cambridge: Harvard University Press, 1965) linked contemporary business practice to the age of the industrial revolution. David S. Landes, *The Unbound Prometheus: Technological Change and Industrial Development in Western Europe from 1750 to the Present* (Cambridge: Cambridge University Press, 1969) powerfully focused the attention of the historical community on the role of technology in the industrial revolution while providing an important model of comparative history. Although Landes extends his analysis to the continent, the British paradigm is at the heart of his account of economic development. Many present-day scholars rely heavily on Landes' account. For a sense of where the scholarly interpretation of the British industrial revolution is today, the essential sources are Joel Mokyr, ed., *The British Industrial Revolution: An Economic Perspective*, 2nd edition (Boulder, CO: Westview Press, 1999) and Roderick Floud and Paul Johnson, eds., *The Cambridge Economic History of Modern Britain, Vol. 1: Industrialisation, 1700–1860* (Cambridge: Cambridge University Press, 2004).

The industrial revolution spread its tentacles all over the world. Kenneth Pomeranz, *The Great Divergence: China, Europe, and the Making of the Modern World Economy* (Princeton: Princeton University Press, 2000) undermined the complacency of insular scholars of Europe or the United States. He and R. Bin Wong, *China Transformed: Historical Change and the Limits of the European Experience* (Ithaca, NY: Cornell University Press, 1997) forced scholars to make more rigorous comparisons. Joseph E. Inikori, *Africans and the Industrial Revolution in England: A Study in International Trade and Economic Development* (Cambridge: Cambridge University Press, 2002) presents a powerful argument about the exploitative nature of the British industrial revolution that, in many ways, parallels that of Thompson. The impact of Western industrialization and imperialism on another continent can be examined through the contrasting, sadly venerable accounts of Walter Rodney, *How Europe Underdeveloped Africa* (Washington, DC: Howard University Press, 1982) and Lewis H. Gann and Peter Duigan, *The Burden of Empire: An Appraisal of Western Colonialism in Africa South of the Sahara* (Stanford, CA: Hoover Institution Press, 1967). A pleasurable and informative read for those interested in business practice and technological change in the United States is Judith A. McGaw, *Most Wonderful Machine: Mechanization and Social Change in Berkshire Paper Making 1801–1885* (Princeton: Princeton University Press, 1987). A good introduction to the differing national experiences of industrialization around the globe with an up-to-date bibliography is Jeff Horn, Leonard N. Rosenband, and Merritt Roe Smith, eds., *Reconceptualizing the Industrial Revolution* (Cambridge, MA: MIT Press, 2007).

Today, many people do not want to know about books or articles in periodicals like the flagship *Journal of Modern History*, they want to know what might be available online. While researching and writing this book, I constantly looked to see what could be found through GOOGLE, other search engines and more specialized sites. I also followed up on all the extensive internet sources listed in James E. McClellan III and Harold Dorn, *Science and Technology in World History* published in 1999. I was often surprised, both positively and negatively, by what I found. For those who desire further information from an encyclopedia, the sixth edition of the Columbia Encyclopedia is available at http://www.bartleby.com/65/; the various search engine versions and contributor-based resources like Wikipedia are horrible at best and dangerous at worst. Do not waste your time with them. The amount of false information and mistakes was staggering. Even nominally monitored sites collecting information on British history like http://www.victorianweb.org/ and http://www.cottontimes.co.uk/ had numerous factual errors and problematic assertions to go along with some valuable materials and information. I found some useful material on various places on the site for A Vision of Britain through Time (http://vision.edina.ac.uk/index.jsp). Some sites purportedly for instructors like http://www.teachersfirst.com were so bad that it was laughable, while the account of women workers in http://www.womeninworldhistory.com/lesson7.html might be helpful to some. In the end, unless an online source is accredited to a reputed institution such as the Museum of Textile History (http://www.athm.org/), the British Public Record Office (PRO) (http://www.nationalarchives.gov.uk/) or a known scholar with some sort of affiliation that you recognize it should be avoided. Reliable information beyond a brief introduction and what amounted to encyclopedia articles in html was also nearly impossible to find. Beginners will find separating the wheat from the chaff of historical materials (some real and some not) on the Web almost impossible. The library remains the best place to find reliable accurate accounts of historical events.

Disappointment also dogged my search for images. Since photography was in its infancy during the age of the industrial revolution, there are almost no contemporary photographs. Although woodcuts, drawings, and paintings representing industrial topics abound, I found few of them on the Web. Three essential resources are the American Memory project at the Library of Congress (http://memory.loc.gov/ammem/index.html), the Making of America site at Cornell University (http://cdl.library.cornell.edu/moa/), and History Matters at the Center for History and New Media at George Mason University (http://historymatters.gmu.edu/). In addition to primary sources including some images, this important site also maintains an up-to-date listing of reviewed and annotated Web sites dealing with American history. The New York Public Library's Digital Collection (http://digitalgallery.nypl.org/nypldigital/index.cfm), the Perry-Castañeda Library Map Collection at the University of Texas at Austin (http://www.lib.utexas.edu/maps/) and David Rumsey's Map Collection (www.davidrumsey.com) along with the valuable Internet Modern History Sourcebook for primary documents produced by Fordham University (http://www.fordham.edu/halsall/mod/modsbook.html) are all useful resources for students and scholars.

For more specialized information, consult the appropriate professional association or the internet discussion group hosted by H-Net. Here are some reliable places to start on economic history (http://eh.net/) and the history of technology (http://invention.smithsonian.org/). The industrial revolution is one of the most important developments in world history: by using reliable portal sites and following their links, finding out more can be relatively easy and fun.

Index